I've travelled the world twice over,
Met the famous: saints and sinners,
Poets and artists, kings and queens,
Old stars and hopeful beginners,
I've been where no-one's been before,
Learned secrets from writers and cooks
All with one library ticket
To the wonderful world of books.

© JANICE JAMES.

HIGH HOPES

In 1960, at the age of nineteen, Norman
Croucher lost both legs below the knee
in a railway accident. In his determination to fight back, he walked from John
O' Groats to Land's End for Oxfam on
his new metal legs. Then he turned his
attention to climbing—an interest for
which his appetite had been whetted just
before his accident. His is a story of grit,
patience, ingenuity and humour; his
refusal to give in will give delight and
inspiration to all who read this book.

NORMAN CROUCHER

High Hopes

Complete and Unabridged

ULVERSCROFT
Leicester

First printed 1976

First Large Print Edition
published October 1979
by arrangement with
Hodder & Stoughton Ltd
London

British Library CIP Data

Croucher, Norman
  High hopes.—Large print ed.
  (Ulverscroft large print series: non-fiction).
  1. Croucher, Norman
  2. Physically handicapped—Great Britain
  —Biography 3. Mountaineers—Great Britain
  —Biography
  I. Title
  796.5'22'0924   GV199.92.C/

ISBN 0-7089-0361-4

Published by
F. A. Thorpe (Publishing) Ltd
Anstey, Leicestershire
Printed in England

FOREWORD

I WAS delighted to be asked to contribute the foreword to this important book. Norman Croucher is a disabled young man whom I admire for his determination, perseverance, courage and abiding good humour. He has achieved many remarkable goals. What he has achieved may well be within the reach of readers of this book. But I wonder how many readers, even without his handicaps, would have had the courage to succeed as well as Norman Croucher has done? We read in this book of his love for outdoor pursuits—for walking, canoeing, sailing, cross-country skiing—above all of his great love of climbing. To stand on the top of the Matterhorn and to look down at the world below is the dream of many of us. Yet few of us will ever realise this dream. Norman Croucher has done so.

I hope his book will be very widely read for it shows how, with keen personal endeavour, there can be triumph over even the most severe handicaps. Such triumph is often impossible without the support and encouragement of family and friends. In Norman Croucher's case, the love and devotion of his wife Judy cannot go unrecognised. Without her faith and constant encouragement, his tasks would have been even more daunting. I honour them both for achieving so much together.

Given the right attitude of mind, life can be exciting and rewarding to the handicapped person and he, in turn, can inspire others to greater achievement. This is one reason why facilities to extend the opportunities of handicapped people, not least their opportunities for recreation, were included in the Chronically Sick and Disabled Persons Act. It was my hope when the Act became law, as it is now, that local authorities will never regard recreational opportunities as less important than other forms of help for handicapped people.

I respect and pay warm tribute to the many people who have helped Norman Croucher to realise his aims. Without their fellowship, his potentialities might never have been recognised. What he has proved is that disabled people can be much more than spectators, indeed, that they can be successful leaders in their chosen fields. In thanking Norman for his absorbing book, I wish him every success in everything else he sets out to do. Long may he be an inspiration to us all.

Alfred Morris, MP, Minister for the Disabled

"There's nobody like him. His extraordinary achievements have earned him a place in climbing history."

Chris Bonington

"I am sure that many people, both able-bodied and disabled will be inspired by this book to attempt a sport or recreation that previously they had thought was beyond them, and which will provide the challenge and motivation for an exciting and fulfilled life. The battle to overcome a handicap is greatly enhanced through leading as normal a life as possible, and encourages the spirit and determination that is also necessary to be successful in sport.

The Sports Council fully recognises the needs and demands of disabled sportsmen and now new facilities are designed with their requirements in mind, and existing facilities are being adapted where necessary. Many courses are arranged to encourage participation at all levels.

I'm sure that the author's example will do much to encourage the readers to 'get out and have a go'—there's lots of fun and excitement to be had by all. Our thanks should go to Norman Croucher for showing us the way, and allowing us to share his moments of personal triumph."

Alan Pascoe

"From now on whenever I reflect on the dizzy heights I once scaled in the football world, I will do so with more humility. For I achieved what I achieved with the help of ten colleagues, plus every physical advantage.

Norman Croucher, on the other hand, has achieved his miracle alone. However much he credits those around him, however much he dismisses his disability, the story he tells so vividly is a story of one man's marvellous resolution and spirit.

In many ways it reads like something out of *Boys Own,* that is until you keep reminding yourself that this man Croucher actually exists and has actually encountered all these 'adventures in the mountains.'

His one fault is his modesty summed up perfectly in the title *High Hopes.* To me this story is about an 'Impossible Dream'. "

Bob Wilson

"At the beginning of this fascinating book Norman Croucher writes, 'I chose to seek adventure in the mountains', his achievements on some of the great mountains of the Alps indicate that he did indeed find adventure. The routes he tackled on the Matterhorn, Jungfrau and the West Flank of the Eiger would have tested many able-bodied people. Norman Croucher will have a unique place in mountain lore; his courage, determination and grit are without equal. He is an inspiration to us all."

Joe Brown

I chose to seek adventure in the mountains, and have not been disappointed.

The routes on which I struggled may appear tame to experienced, hard climbers, but there seems no need to apologise for that.

Maybe this story will lure some people towards the mountains and cliffs, but I don't attempt to persuade them. The decision, and the responsibility to protect their own lives, rests with them.

N.C.

1

THE year was 1960. I wanted to climb but had lost my legs below the knees in a railway accident. People said it was a crazy idea, to think about climbing with artificial legs, but that hope was cherished throughout convalescence. Two days on a rock climbing course before I lost my legs had planted the seed of enthusiasm. That course was months before, as if in another life.

Before being fitted with artificial legs I got about with crutches on a pair of pylons, which resemble peg legs. What a dizzy experience, using pylons for the first time after ten weeks in bed. I managed only twenty or thirty Bambi paces before slumping down on a chair. But improvement came steadily with practice.

At the convalescent home a visiting surgeon enquired each week about my progress. When at first I walked a hundred yards he told me he knew a seventy-year-old lady who had two pylons and could go twice as far. If I went up and down the stairs five times his old lady had been up and down stairs five times but on a flight twice as long as the one I practised on. If I walked a quarter of a mile his lady could walk half a mile. For some time we went on in this way with his lady Tarzan doing at least twice what I did.

Before long I joined the small group of men who hobbled each day with crutches or sticks three hundred yards to the local park, where the boating lake was the big attraction. We rowed about contentedly in the sunshine of late summer, but were soon barred from the boats for using crutches as punt poles.

On the way back from the park one day I noticed a tree, no more than five or six yards high. Could I climb or not? Scrambling over a low fence to reach the tree, I pulled up with both arms on a branch and brought the rubber disc of a pylon to rest on the rough bark of another branch, as thick as my arm. Swinging the second pylon up beside its partner, I stretched to hold as high as I could on the trunk. It was not hard to heave up again and raise the pylons one after the other to a higher branch, and a little higher still. What I had hoped was confirmed, that the simplest movements of easy climbing were possible if I relied more on my arms than my legs for power. The placement of each lifeless pylon had to be made with extreme care to avoid a slip, but wanting to climb was not so silly after all. A pair of crutches discarded on the grass added strength to that aspiration.

On the day after I had been up my tree the thin, bespectacled surgeon appeared on his rounds.

"How far did you get yesterday, young man?"

The staff nurse answered for me.

"Ten feet," she said. "Upwards. Up a tree."

The surgeon nodded, smiled and said, "Well done."

We never heard about his lady again, but even though she probably never existed she had spurred me along the way. Soon I left the convalescent home and went to live with my parents in Cornwall.

In those days there was a delay of many months before artificial limbs were fitted. Mine were ready just before Christmas, seven months after losing my real legs. The hard work of learning to walk on them began, first with two crutches or sticks, then by moving from one piece of furniture to the next without support from crutches or sticks. Gradually

I could take longer and longer journeys between the furniture, measured first in paces, three, four, five, and then in tens of paces. In a day or two I made short expeditions out of doors with crutches. A few more days passed before I could launch myself away from the security of a wall or a door handle to totter without sticks or crutches along the rough lane which ran beside our house. I fell occasionally but came to no harm. Most of the time I followed the advice of a physiotherapist, to concentrate on developing a good walking action rather than dispensing with crutches and sticks too soon. Following two walking training sessions at a hospital the physiotherapist decided that I needed no external encouragement to practise, so future appointments were cancelled. Being young and single I was motivated to get out and about. Youth helped in many ways: my strength and balance were good and if my stumps bled from too much walking they healed quickly. I was fortunate to be twenty years old.

Eight weeks of walking practice went by and I took a job away from home in a laboratory so I would be forced to fend for myself. I had found the job after an unsuccessful try at the local labour exchange.

"As a disabled person," the man there had told me, "you could be a lift operator, a car park attendant, a tailor or a watchmaker."

It must have been obvious that the limited choice offered was not received with enthusiasm and I think the man took offence. Whether by mistake or in retaliation I don't know (I suspect the latter), but a week later a green card from the labour exchange came by post. It informed me that there was a vacancy I might be interested in, quite close to home—as a hod carrier on a building site!

Each day I waddled a third of a mile to the laboratory, back to my digs at lunch time, again to work and once more to the digs when work was finished. At first, even with two sticks those four trips were all I could manage in a day, but as time went on the distances increased, for a while with one stick, then with none.

There would be no point in saying that walking did not hurt. The right stump gave more and more pain as each day dragged on, until by evening I was exhausted. If both stumps had been like the left one progress would have been more rapid and without pain. For two and a half years I tried various methods of easing the nagging pain in the right stump, caused simply by the pressure of the protective sock on the flesh and bone at the end of the stump. I had to terminate a teacher training course prematurely because even the limited amount of standing involved in that form of work was too much at the time. How strange that seems now, looking back. Stupidly, I did not consult a doctor about this severe discomfort but just accepted it as an inevitable consequence. A less stubborn "grin and bear it" attitude would have saved me from a lot of pain. When I finally found a solution (sewing a piece of tape to the end of the stump sock so it could be pulled away from the bone) the release from the pain was so marked that my walking range instantly increased by three or more times. So ended two and a half years; such pain made the remaining discomfort easier to bear.

During those two and a half years, experiments with various sporting and leisure pursuits soon showed that plenty of active pastimes were still available. The popular dance of the time was the twist; I found to my great pleasure one night that the dance was possible, although there was one drawback—when I got home I discovered that some of the rivets had popped out of my legs! Skating was hard and I seemed to spend more time on my back on the ice than actually skating. Riding a scooter: not difficult. After falling off one day I finished up with a large dent in one leg, and it was likely that if the leg had been real it would have been broken or very painful. A camping and hitch-hiking holiday took me through France, Belgium, Germany and Luxembourg. Gliding and cycling proved to be possible too. But always, always on my mind was climbing. Several months after the ascent of the tree I scrambled awkwardly over a rough grey rock on a beach. Yes, climbing was on, so I wrote to a climbing instructor, Jim Smith, and we arranged to meet. He was thin and agile, and in his forties. As we sat in his car, ready to drive the few miles from his home to the sea cliffs, I mentioned my legs for the first time and said I would like to climb. I felt it was likely that he would refuse to help.

"We can soon find out what you can do," he said, and away we went to the cliffs. It seemed that the question of saying no had not entered his head.

A walk of a few hundred yards down a rough track through the gorse brought us to the cliffs on the Atlantic coast. I walked behind Jim because in those days I stumbled and fell quite often on rough ground. And that's just what happened a couple of times, but I don't think Jim saw. Once on the rocks I would be all right because I could steady myself with my hands. For some years I was to find that moving over rough country was very exhausting.

Jim was calm, patient, thoughtful, and above all sufficiently skilled to be confident that he could choose relatively safe situations for me to experiment in; to go with an expert was the way to find out without too much danger. So we started on little bits of rock only sixty or seventy feet high. The rock was steep but easy because of plentiful holds for hands and feet in the form of ledges, cracks and jutting knobs of grey granite. I was a real beginner. The two days on a rock climbing course before I lost my legs helped me to decide that I could still climb, but when it came to performing the movements I had to start from scratch. Jim always went first and held the rope from above in case I fell.

It was essential to look down frequently at my boots to make sure that they had not moved as they were inclined to slip from small toe holds. The placement of the lower extremities clearly had to be very precise. Steadiness of movement was of the essence, even more than for an able-bodied climber. When in a position where I had to stand with a leg bent a little at the knee, the strain on the thigh caused it to tremble, with the result that the boot was inclined to slip. If both legs were bent the effect was increased greatly, and I hung on with shivering thighs in hot and cold weather alike. Another minor problem was that if I raised a foot to a hold only as high as a chair seat I lacked the leg strength to step up. Arms had to provide almost all of the power, whereas the usual climber gains most power from his legs. A further difficulty was the limited bend of the knees, not much over ninety degrees. Most frustrating of all was my inability to move the feet from the ankles to left or right, up or down, to fit nicely on holds. The feet just stuck out rigidly at attention, pointing straight forward. In addition, I lost several inches in reach through not being able to stand on tiptoe.

So there were several hindrances which could have been used as excuses if I did not want to climb, but none which really made climbing impossible. Rather than prevent participation, my physical condition only set limits on the difficulty of the routes which I could manage. Judging from the little climbing experience I had prior to losing my legs, the major differences were that I would now need to concentrate much more, and obviously progress would be very strenuous by comparison.

Under Jim's guidance I learned at weekends, while wriggling up rock chimneys, clinging to faces with a leg and an arm jammed comfortingly in a crack, or hauling myself mostly by arm strength over bulges. There were no easy solutions to my special problems; only practice and trying harder could bring improvement.

It was a special day for me when Jim suggested we should climb Bosigran Ridge, seven hundred feet up and down, up and down over a series of pinnacles which stretched up and inland from the sea. At that time I had to climb half of the route then leave it by an easy way off to a path running along the bottom of the ridge. The following weekend we returned to do the remainder of the ridge, and I remember the pleasure I felt at completing the route. I could not begin to compare with the speed of able-bodied climbers for I had taken at least four times as long; but what did speed matter? I had been on the route and I had enjoyed it.

What would have happened if Jim had said no when first I asked for his help? I might not have climbed at all. So I was very grateful, for largely because of him the adventure had begun.

Over the next few years I was drawn to a few cliffs in Britain. In those early, tentative years on rock it seemed that while many cliffs and outcrops were accessible, mountains put up barriers which would for ever exclude me. It was not that the climbing was hard on mountains, for often it was the opposite; but the journeys were long. The combination of a march from the nearest road followed by a lengthy climb seemed too ambitious to contemplate. So nine years of rock climbing went by with hardly a thought about mountains, except for nagging regrets that they were not for me. Then, one day in 1969, on a sketch map of Snowdonia, the name and position of a mountain caught my eye. The peak, Tryfan, was marked as just over three thousand feet high and from the roughly drawn map I judged the summit to be within a mile and a half of the nearest road. Could I climb long enough to reach that summit? And descend safely? It seemed possible, just possible. There was one fact in my favour at the time: the month was February, snow lay deep on the mountain, and cold conditions suited me because the stumps of my legs were less inclined to injury when cool and free of perspiration. I had climbed short rock routes for a few hours at a time. Would a mountain journey of a few hours be much different? If I attempted Tryfan I could decide as I went along whether I should climb the mountain or merely see how far I could go. Ambition would have to be tempered by caution, and as long as a continuous assessment was made of whether I should turn back or go on I would not climb too far. The summit was a carrot but I was likely to get only part way towards it.

"How about seeing if I can get up Tryfan?"

The question was directed at Peter, a climbing pal.

"All right."

Off we went and slept in Peter's mini-van in a lay-by at the foot of Tryfan. It was fine the next day.

In summer the ascent of Tryfan by our route is a walk and scramble; when covered in snow it is a more serious proposition. To start with there was half an hour's easy trudge through ankle-deep snow on the gentle lower slopes. If you look at it from the right direction, and use your imagination, Tryfan looks a bit like a short, very fat lizard-like creature lying with its tail pointing north and its head looking south. The snow steepened to twenty-five degrees until we reached the Heather Terrace, a prominent rock fault running almost the length of the east face of the mountain in a gradual upward incline from north to south, or from the lizard's tail to its shoulders.

We each had an ice-axe; they would be our brakes if we slipped. In places we crossed gaps where a slip would have sent us tumbling a long way, but the chances of such a fall were remote. Still, with a novice like me around we could not afford to take risks, and I felt the need for us to be roped together when we passed exposed spots. At such times Peter positioned himself so he could hold me on the rope if I fell.

Each hour was punctuated by short rests. As the hundreds of paces added up I expected pain to signal that the stumps had had enough, but they remained cool and uninjured.

Icicles hung in huge, clear fangs. Chunks of ice dislodged by people above slithered and hissed past. Groups of climbers overtook us from time to time. Proceeding slowly up the gradual incline for an hour, two hours, three hours and more, we reached the far end of the Heather Terrace at two o' clock. Now the way went northwards, from the lizard's shoulder and across the spine of its hunched back towards the highest hump, the summit. The latest time to turn back, we agreed, was half-past three, whether we had attained the summit or not.

Haste led us to turn north sooner than we should have. Facing us was rock which in summer conditions would have been an easy scramble, but summer was a long way off and ice hindered climbing. Had we taken the trouble to look we would have found an easy way within a hundred feet.

Pete went ahead and had to climb almost the full hundred and twenty feet length of the rope before he could find somewhere to belay, that is, tie himself to a rock projection so he would not be pulled down if I slipped. By the time I had followed him up that section I was exhausted, and could do no more than crawl on all fours through the snow for a few yards. Wedged between two rocks, I rested in a rock armchair with a soft snow cushion.

"Be all right in a couple of minutes, Pete."

He asked the time.

"Three o' clock. Only half an hour before we turn back. Weather still looks good."

Hopes of making the summit faded considerably.

"I'll just scout ahead while you take it easy," Pete said, tramping on. A hundred feet above he went out of sight behind rock. Two minutes later he came into view again, shouting and waving his arms.

"It's only a couple of hundred feet to the top from where I'm standing! Just a walk!"

We hurried on to stand within five minutes beside Adam and Eve, the two big rocks which crown the summit. We grinned and giggled like schoolboys in a joke shop. It was a small mountain, but at least it was a mountain. I felt an elation which I was to be moved to seek again at the top of many peaks.

Two climbers told us it was time to be getting down because it was nearly half past four. By a stroke of luck my watch had broken at three o' clock and we had climbed for almost an hour longer than planned, taking six hours just to get up. If it were not for that breakage we would not have climbed Tryfan.

We had extra food and clothing for an emergency but did not relish the thought of a night out on the mountain. We scurried back, part of the time slithering on our bottoms and controlling the slide with ice-axes. The whole descent took about two hours, in daylight all the way.

I could hardly believe I had climbed a real mountain and my stumps were not damaged much. Suddenly, a whole new world opened up, though at the time I did not realise how much influence the mountains would have. This was a distinct watershed in life. Higher mountains beckoned, but it seemed advisable first to undergo some form of endurance training to improve my stamina on long treks. A few weeks later I made up my mind to walk the length of Britain, the nine hundred miles from John O' Groats in the north of Scotland to Land's End in Cornwall.

It was frustrating to wait for the cool walking weather at the end of the year. Meanwhile I looked around for sponsors who would donate small amounts of money to Oxfam for each mile covered. The aim was to average ten miles a day but I did not practise beforehand because there would be considerable pain involved in a ten-mile training walk; if I knew how bad the pain was on one day, the prospect of ninety consecutive days would have been discouraging. It was better simply to decide that no matter how long the walk took, it would be completed.

September 18th, 1969. A sunny, windless morning at John o' Groats. I started to walk and almost immediately took the wrong road! After a few hundred yards I realised that the road pointed westwards instead of to the south. Back on the right road, eagerness led me to walk sixteen miles, causing my stumps to split open and bleed in half a dozen places by the end of the day.

The following day was very hot. Within six miles the pain became almost unbearable and I had to call a halt. I felt sick with pain, and disappointed that it had taken more than five hours to move six miles. For someone who planned to walk nine hundred miles it was not an impressive performance.

The first two weeks of walking were filled with pain and the smell of antiseptic ointment. Then my stumps toughened to the punishment they received, though still they broke open quite often. The stumps set the limits. With the walking spread over daylight hours I maintained an average of ten miles a day. To make life easier I put my rucksack on a golf caddy-cart.

For more than a hundred miles the road weaved along close to the choppy sea until, south of Inverness, the highway climbed into wild mountain country. There was snow on the peaks.

A roving evangelist stopped to talk on a quiet stretch of road. I sat on a hedge and he had his back to the highway. Behind him on a transporter a tiny yellow submarine went by—it had been used in a search for the Loch Ness monster. The evangelist was telling me about the meetings he was holding in various Scottish towns and villages when I interrupted.

"There's a yellow submarine going up the road behind you."

He was open-mouthed, wide-eyed and clearly not sure if he was talking to a crazy man who pushed a caddy-cart and imagined yellow submarines on the road, until he turned to confirm what I said was true. I laughed to myself all day about the look on his face.

With the rucksack mounted on a golf caddy-cart I received much bewildered scrutiny while trundling up high streets and along lonely country roads.

Inevitably, one question kept recurring.

"I hope you don't mind me asking, but how did you lose your legs?"

In the planning stage of the walk I had anticipated that this would happen often, and I did not look forward to being asked.

"I was drunk, when I was nineteen, and was run over by a train which cut my legs off."

"Oh!"

That question had to be faced repeatedly because, naturally enough, people were curious. The alternative was to retreat, to hide, to miss a large part of life itself, for the long walk proved to be a link in a chain which led to some delightful climbing experiences. So it had to be put into words, that the fault was mine; how ashamed I was to say that at first. But it was a comfort that as the fault was mine there was no reason for bitterness against any man. To come to terms with the physical and psychological consequences was up to me, and bitterness could only hinder that process.

19

Day after day the ribbon of road stretched relentlessly away into the distance. When I had walked about two hundred and fifty miles I met a man who had run from John o' Groats to Land's End, starting a few days before me. He had taken nineteen days and was hitch-hiking home when we met; he came up and introduced himself because he had heard that someone was pushing a caddy-cart to Land's End. Sitting on the window-sill of a derelict house, we had a long talk. His name was Eric Beard, and he was a keen mountaineer. We exchanged addresses in order to keep in touch and climb together in the Alps. He jotted my name and address in the front of his diary. Several days later he was killed in a motor accident and at the scene of the tragedy the police found his diary—with my name and address on the front page. My wife, Judy, was informed that I was believed to be dead. Fortunately, she knew where I was staying that night and was able to ring to confirm that I was all right.

On the way up the high road over Shap Fell in a gale, stinging rain made it difficult to see. It was a relief to retreat into the little wooden café at the top of the hill. Walking up to the counter, I was puzzled by a strange, slopping sound. When I sat down and lifted one foot to tie a shoelace the cause became evident at once: water poured from the hollow leg. Driving rain had filled both legs.

Outside the café again, the wind continued to bluster. On the rocky left verge an embankment gave some protection from the gale so I chose that side. Dragging the caddy-cart over rocks and through mud was a slow business and the gale grew worse. Suddenly the caddy-cart and rucksack, weighing together over thirty pounds, rose in the air as the wind took them. I hung on, then my feet were off the ground. I was airborne too, with body flying parallel to the ground! Releasing the caddy-cart, I grabbed at a big boulder but was pushed away by the force of the wind. The whole incident lasted only seconds before my feet were back on the ground; then I realised I was on all fours in the road with traffic passing close by. With a quick crawling motion I was soon back on the verge where the rucksack and caddy-cart lay. The wind died away and allowed an easy walk down the valley.

Through Kendal, Lancaster, Preston and Wigan. On the way out of Wigan the right stump began to swell. After a mile I had to rest, then again after half a mile. Before long there were stops every fifty yards as the throbbing pain grew worse. On that day I managed only four miles, and had to rest the whole of the next day.

With two-thirds of the journey completed my stumps still split and bled at times, but less often than at the beginning of the walk. Through Tewkesbury, Gloucester, Bristol and Taunton I plodded at an old man's pace. The average daily distance remained at a little more than ten miles although at times I pushed on for fourteen or fifteen miles. Sometimes for a week or more there was no escape from the rain or from water splashed up by traffic.

On entering the county of Cornwall there were less than a hundred miles to go. I ambled through the little village where my father was born and from where he was taken to live in the local workhouse as a boy. He always worked hard and when my two sisters and I reached our teens he achieved an ambition: after several years as a butcher he had made enough money to buy a small farm.

The walk took me past Redruth Grammar School where I spent six years: I remembered evenings spent training with the school gymnastic display team, cold afternoons in the mud and water on cross-country runs, Saturdays on the rugby field. None of those sports would suit me again but two activities I did at school I can still take part in: shooting and gliding. I recall that the first time I fired five rounds with a .303 rifle I had not a single hole in my target and the boy next to me fired five rounds and had nine holes in his. I had been aiming at the wrong target! Gliding did not start well either, as the instructor's slowly spoken words after my first landing indicated: "Son, if you make another landing like that you'll be sitting on your arse in the grass in the middle of a pile of firewood." But I improved and flew solo.

Not far from the school I could see the farmhouse where we had lived, standing out high on a hill. The granite outcrops of that hill were my earliest training ground, where I climbed occasionally without rope or companions in my teens, as anyone of that age might. The farm was only thirty acres, unprofitable, and my father had been forced to sell the place. He bought a van and ran a door-to-door butcher's business in the country.

Trudging the length of the spine of Cornwall, I reached Land's End after three months on the road. A reception at the St. Ives Guildhall, complete with Mayor, Mayoress and town band, signalled the end of the walk.

The walk raised over £1,000 for Oxfam and at the same time toughened me for lengthy mountain treks. The days of pus-filled swellings, and raw patches of flesh became less common because of the hardening effect of the walk on my stumps.

More climbing in Britain followed, then with a friend, Mike, I headed for Switzerland. We had in mind to try the Jungfrau, 13,642 feet (4,158 metres), and its neighbour, the Mönch, 13,449 feet (4,099 metres). Though not difficult by mountaineering standards, I considered that the Mönch and Jungfrau would stretch me to my reasonable limits. The routes started from the Jungfraujoch Hotel, over eleven thousand feet high and served by a mountain railway.

There was bad news when we got there: a severe winter had left deep snow which was too soft to cross without skis between the Jungfraujoch and the Jungfrau. Even if one used skis to approach the mountain, the combination of the heavy snowfall and a hot summer left the mountain covered in soft, dangerous snow. It would gradually avalanche and melt away but it could take two weeks before the route was safe. However, the Mönch was accessible by the south-east ridge.

At four o'clock in the morning we slouched from the dormitory into faint light, where the chill air jolted us to alertness. The dawn start would give a few hours climbing on frozen snow before the heat of the day turned it slushy. The topmost five hundred feet of the Mönch were swathed in mist.

It was a mile over crisp snow to the base of the south-east ridge, then a plod of three or four hundred feet up a snow slope of twenty degrees. The route became steeper, rocky in many places, and the ridge sloped away sharply on either side.

Soon the snow was softening, making movement more difficult. For hour after hour we dragged ourselves up snow ridges and over easy steps of rock. I was very slow. Because of the mist we could not judge how far above the summit was. There would be a rope-length of snow to climb, and another, and another, as the mountain revealed itself only a little at a time through the thin veil. The ridge was too obvious for us to lose the way, even in mist. We saw no one else.

Just after nine o'clock we mounted a broad shoulder of snow from which the summit was suddenly visible, five minutes' walk or less away across a rising pathway of snow. On either side the snow plunged away steeply, making me feel as if I were walking a plank high up.

"Too dangerous," Mike said.

"No. Come on. It's all right."

We went on with great care, to within a hundred yards of the summit, then halted. We had come to a place where we would have to walk across a huge cornice, a mass of wind-blown snow which curves over like a wave about to break—the underside is hollow. The wind had spent all winter gradually building it up. Often you can walk safely below a cornice on the side which is not overhanging if you pick a line which is below the level of that snow which will be carried away if the cornice collapses. The cornice we faced was several yards long and wide, and to keep a safe distance from it we would have been forced down a very steep slope of soft snow. Too soft. It looked dangerous. The summit was a hundred yards away and less than fifty feet higher than we were. I argued with Mike, against my own better judgment, that we should go on, but I knew all the time that we should not and would not. We did what was sensible and turned back.

Halfway down the ridge three ascending climbers went by. They were the only people we saw on the mountain that day. Crossing the glacier, we sank up to our knees at each step, and did not arrive back at the hotel until eleven hours after leaving. I slept and rested on a bunk for fifteen hours; that was an indication of how much one comparatively easy mountain took out of me.

In August I was back on the Mönch with a guide. Much of the snow had disappeared by that time of the year; where the steepest snow had lain there was now easy rock. In three and a half hours we were on the summit. What a foretaste of pleasures to come!

Another guide, Hans, agreed to go with me up the Jungfrau three days later. So at four in the morning we walked south-westwards over undulating snow and between crevasses on the glacier at the foot of the mountain. Soon, with crampons strapped to boots, we commenced to climb a thousand feet of snow varying in steepness between thirty degrees and about fifty degrees. The crampons, metal frameworks of spikes, stuck out under our boots and made it easier to move over ice and hard snow. I felt the advantage of being reasonably well acclimatised to the thin air after five or six days at high altitude. Several people overtook us.

By the time we reached the Rottal Sattel, a saddle between the Jungfrau and the neighbouring Rottal mountain, we had risen about fourteen hundred feet above the Jungfraujoch. We rested for a few minutes before turning to the north-west, passing a place from which, Hans told me, five people fell a thousand feet to their deaths in two climbing accidents on consecutive days in 1969.

The route went only rarely over patches of bare rock. Farther up, climbers were cutting steps in the frozen snow, causing small chunks to skim by on the frozen surface. We climbed with crampons over rock as well as snow and ice; taking them off and strapping them on could have wasted a lot of time.

Time sped by on the mist-shrouded mountain. We came upon a group of more than twenty mountaineers resting on some rocks, and suddenly, unexpectedly, I realised that we were at the top. The climb took less time than I expected: we had reached the summit in a little over four hours.

I took a long time to descend on soft snow and Hans was clearly displeased at how I managed. For some years to come, soft snow would be my greatest mountain problem.

From the first rock climb with Jim Smith in Cornwall to reaching the summit of the Jungfrau nearly a decade had gone by. It took that long to turn a disabled man into a mountaineer, and then only into a beginner. I thought at the time that I had reached a target and a terminus. But the call of the mountains is strong, and far from being at a terminus I was only a short way along the journey. I had dabbled with peaks and now I found it hard to manage without them. My mountaineering life was just beginning.

Climbing became increasingly important and soon my wife Judy and I agreed that my career would have to take second place for a while to two ambitions: at the same time as progressing as a climber I hoped, particularly through writing, to do something towards creating opportunities for other disabled people in outdoor pursuits. I wanted them to have the chance to find the enjoyment I had found, not necessarily in climbing but in any outdoor activity they chose, like camping, rambling, angling, gliding or canoeing. Competitive sports for people with certain handicaps had been promoted for several years, but, with few exceptions, non-competitive sports had been neglected. It was time for suitable non-competitive sports to be promoted too, not instead of, but as well as, competitive games.

Judy remained in a Civil Service job while for a few years I was employed in the Post Office, at an accommodation agency, as a social worker, in the Civil Service, washing up in a hotel, at any work which would fit in with the timetable. Often I felt uncomfortable about this way of life but Judy never wavered in her conviction that for a few years climbing and the creation of opportunities for other disabled people by writing should take precedence. She was very patient and understanding with her restless husband over several uncertain years. A prime consideration was to allow sufficient free time in summer to train and if necessary to wait for the right weather conditions; the latter proved to be a key factor in the events which followed. Looking back I can see that greater attention paid to earnings, career and security could have cost me the dearest ambitions, but it was not always easy to see that at the time. Similarly, if Judy had been more materialistic I might have failed in those ambitions. What a change it was from my former way of life as a social worker for four and a half years at St. Martin-in-the-Fields Church in London. Now gaps in my employment and periods on low wages meant that we had very little money, but we saved what we could towards climbing trips. Our home was a bed-sitter in Ealing, London. A car was out of the question, and in one way this was good because I was forced to walk more. Perhaps we were materially poor at times, but only by comparison within our consumer society. Judy was happy with our arrangements, whereas many times I questioned whether I should place more importance on regular employment and career prospects. But mostly we felt as if we had no choice, that it was inevitable that our lives would take a certain course.

2

NO one doubts that mountains may be dangerous places. To move without mishap is the art the mountaineer must learn. He needs stamina, the right equipment, route-finding ability, good companions and technical climbing skill, and it was in the first and last of these requirements that I found myself more limited than the able-bodied climber. The John o' Groats to Land's End walk was an attempt to improve the first, and it was my hope that climbing skill would increase with practice. At the beginning of my climbing life rock climbs were graded according to their difficulty: Easy, Moderate, Difficult, Very Difficult, Severe, Very Severe. Modern equipment and techniques have led to the introduction in recent years of one more grade. I was no agile monkey: climbs up to Very Difficult were within reach if I pushed myself hard. Improvement in rock-climbing ability would bring greater flexibility on the mountains, and the next grade to attempt was Severe.

With this in mind Peter and I planned a day's climbing at Churchill Rocks, a limestone outcrop on the Bristol to Bridgwater road. The outcrop has been quarried to form an amphitheatre with walls of a hundred feet. Trees, tangled bushes, grasses and other small plants crowd the floor and rim. I liked it because there were no other climbers around.

A huge slab, lying back at an angle of forty-five to fifty degrees to the horizontal, caught our interest. We consulted the guide-book: Left Hand Slab—three Just Severe (or Mild Severe) routes, i.e. at the easier end of the Severe grade. The routes looked deceptively easy. I had climbed Moderate and Difficult and Very Difficult routes which were vertical, yet here was a Severe climb which was nowhere steeper than sixty degrees. A lack of holds on the smooth rock accounted for the grade. Within a few yards was another slab at about the same angle but it had lots of holds and was graded Moderate.

My choice: the Just Severe route called Right Hand route which ran straight up the slab a few feet from its right edge. If you imagine a steep roof, ninety feet from top to bottom and made of one piece of grey limestone, you will have a rough picture of the climb. Peter climbed up an easy route, found a good belay at an oak tree, and called for me to climb.

The first ten feet were not difficult because the rock was quite rough, but from then on most of the holds were only big enough for one or two fingertips or a tiny portion of a boot toe—and there were few holds to be found in any case. Some of the time it was necessary to press my palms flat on the rock and rely on the friction to prevent me sliding down. By leaning forward in roughly the position of someone doing press-ups, but with fingers pointing down the slab rather than forwards, the palms were forced hard against the rock. With real feet and flexible footwear I could have kept a large area of each sole on the rock as well, but as it was I had to balance precariously on the front edges of the toes of my boots.

There was no sign of the customary flowing style of the experienced climber; instead there were long, strenuous pauses as I hung on and scrutinised the rock to work out where to move next. Then, tentative reaches of hands and feet, to be pressed against the rock, more often than not failed to hold. My weight would be thrown on three barely existent holds. With palms flat on the rock, arms extended, and perhaps the tip of a boot in a navel sized hole, it was as wearing to remain still as to move.

Slowly, I rose twenty feet up the slab. That left seventy feet to go. There was a crack which made a fairly good fingertip hold with four fingertips in place at once. My boots held, and I took a breather.

Upward again. At one point I put my right knee in a shallow pocket in the rock as I couldn't find a foothold for the right foot. Putting knees on rock is considered bad style but it helps sometimes.

Thirty-five feet from the bottom of the slab I was able to put the toes of my boots in a shallow crack and lie against the rock to rest again. My fingertips felt as if they had clawed their way up and my palms stung from being pressed against the rock for friction. It had taken twenty minutes to get less than halfway up a slab which an able-bodied climber might scale in five minutes or less. My muscles were filled with the pain of tiredness.

Two or three minutes rest and I was on the move again. A few feet to the right was the edge of the slab where the rock was cracked and covered in holds. But I had to keep away from those tempting holds if I wanted to complete the Just Severe climb. The holds were a constant reminder that there was an easy way out if I wanted to give up by moving a few feet to the right.

By the time I had climbed sixty feet my arms were trembling from the strain that had been put on them. Two-thirds of the way up—what a pity if the rock became even more bare of holds and caused me to fail. The sky was cloudy, threatening rain. If the rock was wet there would be little chance of finishing.

Advancing a score more feet, I balanced upward with sweat running in my eyes and dripping on the limestone. Ten feet to go! Gradually the route yielded more holds, small but numerous, sufficient dimples to give grip. It was still hard work but the rock looked less unwelcoming than the limestone further down. Five feet to the top! There was grass growing in little cracks. It was easy now and I reached the top of the slab. It took fifty minutes. Yes, fifty—about ten times as long as an able-bodied climber might need. Now, grades are very much matters of opinion, and are not based solely on technical difficulty: the length of climb, looseness of rock, consistency of difficulties and several other factors may be taken into account. But there it was in black and white, in the guide-book: the route I had been up was in the Severe grade. That was progress.

Peter and I swapped places at the oak tree belay, and in a few minutes he went up the route I had taken. There was the difference: he could move easily and quickly. Not only that, he could lead the climb, whereas we thought it would be out of the question for me to go first on anything but the easiest of climbs. Without the protection of the rope from above, the consequences of even a very short fall were likely to be serious. I was later to change my mind though.

Before long it rained and the rock changed its character instantly, becoming slippery. We descended carefully and went home, feeling that the day, though short, had not been wasted.

That was not to be the only Severe route I managed but I remember it well because it was the first.

In the winter of 1970/1 Peter and I tried to decide on a satisfying alpine route which we could manage in the summer. By December the target was fixed: we would attempt a long, high alpine route involving at least two days of climbing. The Jungfrau was a high route, but it was not really satisfying because the climbing started at a high altitude. By climbing for two or three days I would have a chance to complete a much longer climb in the Alps.

We believed that a long route, tackled slowly, could be undertaken by adapting normal climbing methods to my limitations. Many alpine climbs require a full day's activity for an able-bodied climber if he wishes to avoid spending a night in the open at high altitude. Generally, the mountaineer will in a day climb from a hut or some other shelter to the summit of his choice and back again to a bed. Some climbers plan to camp or bivouac at high altitude so they have time to complete longer and harder routes. Bivouacking differs from camping because a normal tent is not used.

I decided that good bivouac equipment could bring many mountain routes within my range and ensure that I never went too far in one day. The idea was to climb just enough in one day, without injury to the stumps, so climbing could be spread over consecutive days. On a number of occasions I had climbed with the stumps split open. The pain had increased the tiredness brought on by hours of activity, and strength and judgment faded. Unfortunately, whenever the skin on the stumps split, climbing brought very rapid deterioration. Bivouacs would change all that.

The mountain which came to mind is well known: the Eiger. I had seen it many times when waiting to climb the Mönch and the Jungfrau. The three mountains stand together, and I had often felt a little disappointment that I could climb two of them, but not the third. The local story is that the Mönch, or Monk, protects the Jungfrau, the Virgin, from the Eiger, or the Ogre. Now it looked as if that third mountain could be within reach. I could acclimatise at the Jungfraujoch, and we could start the climb from the Eiger Glacier station without a hot trek up through the alpine pastures from the valley. Also, I knew some guides in the area and felt that one or more of them might be prepared to climb with me.

I thought two days would be sufficient to scale the Eiger by an easy route in reasonable conditions. The route we had in mind was known as the west flank.

Alpine moutains lie in surrounding areas of

very high pastures and forests, so to climb a ten thousand feet mountain never involves climbing the full ten thousand feet. Generally the mountaineer follows a trail or takes road transport, a mountain railway or a cable car to the highest convenient point before starting to climb. For this reason the height to be climbed on the Eiger west flank, which is over thirteen thousand feet high, is five thousand four hundred feet. Below the starting point of the climbing are the mountain pastures and tourist walking trails.

We bought bivi-bags, polythene sacks large enough to accommodate one or two people, for protection against wind and rain. Used in conjunction with warm clothing or a sleeping bag, a bivi-bag is adequate for quite harsh conditions. Bivouac experience was the next necessity, we decided, so in February we charged off to North Wales. Two days before there were radio announcements about roads blocked with snow in the area. We planned to tramp about the snowy mountains for hours and bivouac at night, but it was not to be. I had 'flu and spent two nights shivering in the bivi-bag under a rock, and one day sitting either on a rock in weak winter sunshine or in a café.

One piece of equipment seemed to be mocking us on the drive home. Sticking out from under a jumble of rucksacks, rope and clothing was an implement we had commandeered to speed up digging a shelter in the snow—my mother-in-law's coal shovel.

Amongst other places I visited for bivouac practice was Bleaklow Hill in the Peak District, where the land rises to about two thousand feet above sea level. It was March 1971.

"Turn right just before the maggot farm," a water-board man directed. "They breed maggots for animals in zoos and pet shops."

I strolled above the sort of valley where Lorna Doone might have walked. A fast stream tumbled down the middle. When in mist I referred to a map and compass. Only a few months previously I had been puzzled by some wildly inaccurate compass bearings I had taken while sitting on a rock in North Wales. The bearings just did not correspond with the map, and differed by as much as twenty degrees. It was some time before I realised the cause—the map was spread on my knees and whenever I held the compass near the map the metal in my legs made the needle deviate.

It was not only in the mountains that the metal legs produced curious results. I once went through a metal detector test at Nice airport in the company of a group of disabled people who had various pieces of metal, such as crutches, calipers and wheelchairs which kept the detector bleeping. The operator was obviously prepared to give only a rapid, token check to everyone in the group. Now, my old-fashioned but strong legs have metal reinforcing bars which run high up the sides of the thighs. As he moved the small detector down the centre of my body the operator was clearly expecting to find metal somewhere or other. When he found it the detector began to bleep and his face took on an expression of disbelief. The detector, poised over my groin, was bleeping about the reinforcing bars, but the operator didn't know that. He looked up with great sympathy on his face, said "Oh, monsieur!" and waved me on. There was no doubt that he had mistaken the nature of my handicap.

Above eighteen hundred feet there were patches of snow. I was soon at Bleaklow Head, 2,061 feet and the highest point around there. The hike amounted to no more than four and a half miles.

42

As night fell the wind grew fierce. I had a meal and huddled up in the bivi-bag. Daylight had almost gone, although it was still possible to see a few yards in the eerie, misty light. The wind screamed and buffeted the rocks. I was really alone.

Suddenly I was startled by a faint ripping sound. The wind masked the noise and made it diffucult to identify. Rip, rip, rip. Or was it scratch, scratch, scratch? Something was moving close by. It sounded alive, whatever it was, and not like something blown about by the wind. It came closer. Scratch, scratch, scratch. Even closer. I had to see what it was. Folding back the bivi-bag, I peered out, and what I saw scared me. Just three feet away was a face! Strange, staring eyes watched me. The white face nodded up and down a little, only two feet above the ground. It looked terrifying in the faint, misty light. Then I realised what it was. The owner of the face, a sheep, was as alarmed as I was. It let out a grunt and ran away.

The next day visibility was cut by mist to thirty yards. In twenty-four hours I met only one party of hikers, a group of four. This was certainly not the place to expect help to appear opportunely in the event of an accident at that time of year. The trip confirmed in my mind that I would not go out alone again.

As I left the Peak District I looked forward to getting home to London. And as I approached Manchester I was reminded that for me city life is only tolerable if mixed with frequent trips to the hills and mountains.

Peter was getting engaged and it seemed to me that his girlfriend was rather nervous about him going to the Eiger. A certain reluctance crept into his attitude in contrast to his former keenness to go. Some people don't worry much when their friends or relations climb, but others become very anxious, and we had to take this into account. Peter's girlfriend didn't climb and it was understandable that she might regard mountaineering as a pointless and dangerous pastime. If that was so, she was more than justified in hoping that Peter would not risk his life on a mountain. So one day I asked him if he really wanted to go, and he agreed that he had changed his mind.

I wrote to Ueli Sommer, the Swiss guide with whom I had climbed the Mönch. He had told me then that he would be prepared to take me on the Eiger and the point of my letter was largely to confirm this. Ueli's reply arrived in May. He said he could go, and suggested taking a porter as well. Ueli also suggested a possible alternative route to the summit but I was not in favour of this because it started high up at the end of the Jungfraujoch railway. The important news was that he would go. If I didn't find another partner in time, I could go to Switzerland and climb with Ueli. He was bound to be in the area most of the summer as he and his wife managed the Jungfraujoch Hotel.

The Eiger was harder than any mountain I had previously tackled and the most stringent safety precautions were necessary: it would be sensible to climb with a professional mountaineer who knew the area well. Someone from the South Wales Mountaineering Club offered me a lift to Switzerland; we met by chance the year before at Jungfraujoch and had kept in touch.

"There are thirteen seats," he said. "The thirteenth one has been booked a few times but the lads who book it keep getting things like broken legs."

"Sounds like it's intended for me. If I break a leg before we go I can change it."

A special point, which other alpinists

would not need to worry about, was the state of repair of my legs. The month before I left for Switzerland I was walking in London when a rivet dropped out of one of my legs. It seemed like a warning, or a protest against the hard labour to which the artificial limbs were frequently subjected. The leg began to creak and I clicked along like a robot. Apart from the annoying sound, it was disturbing to see that it might crack badly if I walked far. Fortunately I was close to St. Martin-in-the-Fields Church at Trafalgar Square, where I had worked for several years. I sought out the church maintenance man, Joe. He examined the leg. Yes, he could fix that, he told me, and the rivet was replaced in a couple of minutes. I was fairly sure that if I had walked far without that emergency repair I would have damaged the limb a good deal. If that happened near the top of a mountain there would be no Joe around to help.

Then, two or three weeks before I was due to go to the Alps another mechanical problem arose. One of my feet came loose and wobbled about. A hasty 'phone call to the limb centre at Roehampton led to an appointment for emergency repairs and Mr. Campbell, my limb-fitter, soon put the matter right.

Although the legs were kept in a good state of repair by the fitters at Roehampton, I could not ignore the fact that breakages could occur on the mountain. I resolved, therefore, to examine the legs closely before and during each long climb and to carry some rivets which I could hammer with a piton hammer or ice-axe. To add strength I bound the metal legs with strong insulation tape around their weakest points, at the tops of the shins. They would stand up to any amount of walking but climbing put abnormal strains on the metal. By wrapping the insulation tape around in much the same way as you might to strengthen a pick handle, the effect was to protect the metal from cracks and to slow the growth of any cracks which might form.

What other differences were there between me and an able-bodied climber? Well, each step would cost me more in energy, I would be slower than an able-bodied man and my stumps would be injured if I went too far in one day—in a way the stumps were my Achilles heel. By planning to bivouac I was bringing the route within my personal limits. At least, that's what I thought.

3

THE packing is finished. I've spent the past hour weighing things on kitchen scales so I can take the minimum possible weight of equipment.

"I'm off now, Ju."

She doesn't try to stop me climbing. What would I do if she did?

"I'm a bit worried, Norm, but I know how much climbing means to you."

An hour later I was waiting at Victoria Station for the mini-bus hired by the South Wales Mountaineering Club. The vehicle arrived and thirteen people filled the seats and struggled to find room for rucksacks and ice-axes.

Within half an hour we had a puncture, so out came the spare wheel. That had two large nails in it already so we had to buy another at a nearby garage.

At half past four the ailing vehicle was halted near Canterbury because one wheel was groaning. We couldn't find out why. Gloom descended on the company and the mini-bus crawled slowly into Dover. There an A.A. man inspected the complaining wheel while the seconds ticked away, bringing close the time of the boat's departure at seven a.m. It was a close thing. The A.A. man adjusted the wheel and while tightening the nuts fell on his head. He picked himself up and said the wheel was all right. There was no time to waste: we all scrambled back into the mini-bus and drove to the boat, leaving the A.A. man a little dazed and sucking his grazed knuckles.

In France we drove with hardly a stop until it was time to camp for the night at Vesoul, quite close to Switzerland.

The next day we reached the outskirts of Basle before having another puncture. The tyre was old and useless, which is a polite version of the description applied by several people to the man who hired out the mini-bus. It took a time to find a garage which could supply another tyre on a Sunday, and it was while we were at the garage that one of the doors came adrift from its hinge.

I felt a bit like a rat leaving a sinking ship when I alighted at Zurich to take a train to Grindelwald, but Zurich was the last point from which I could travel conveniently. As I waved goodbye and the vehicle pulled away from the kerb I wouldn't have been too surprised if it had keeled over. In fact the mini-bus reached its destination on the outward journey and needed to be taken to a garage only once to prevent a wheel falling off. On the return journey, I was told, the cylinder head gasket blew and the transport was abandoned at Dover by all hands.

I went by train to Grindelwald, then took a ticket on the local mountain railway which has the Jungfraujoch Hotel at its terminus. The train clattered up a steep track where the gradient reached twenty-five degrees. Rhododendron bushes and pine slipped by the windows, then there were no more trees or bushes. Rich, green alpine pastures on both sides of the line were speckled with flowers of yellow, pink, red, purple and blue which matched the sky. Cows nodded and their bells rang while they munched, ignoring the train.

Kleine Scheidegg, 6,726 feet (2,061 metres), is the crowded interchange where you take another train for Jungfraujoch. From Kleine Scheidegg the train soon disappears into the four and a half mile tunnel cut right through the Eiger and Mönch. The railway tunnel, opened in 1912, begins at the Eiger Glacier station, a complex of a hotel, husky pens and railway buildings which sprawl along the line. A glacier crevasse was used as a refrigerator for the meat eaten by the hundreds of workers who helped to build the tunnel, and frozen red wine was sold to them by weight. Their labours over fourteen years, involving the deaths of several men, produced a tunnel through which the visitor can rise without effort from the Eiger Glacier station, 7,612 feet (2,320 metres), to the Jungfraujoch, 11,333 feet (3,454 metres), in less than three-quarters of an hour.

Emerging from the tunnel into the Jungfraujoch station is like drawing up in a long, rough-hewn cave about twenty yards wide. Thirty paces from the platform is the mountainside, which you can reach by walking through a lobby. An observation balcony overlooks the fourteen-mile long Aletsch glacier. The Jungfrau stands close by; on this day it was covered on the steep face nearest to the balcony with a sprinkling of snow, smooth and sparkling white like a thin dusting of icing sugar. Near the base of the Jungfrau were the jumbled chunks of ice where two young Swiss climbers had been crushed to death in a huge avalanche two

51

weeks earlier, on the route I had taken twelve months before.

The hotel hangs from the steep mountainside in the way that a fortress might: much of the building is inside the rock. For the visitor there is a restaurant, dormitory and hotel accommodation, a man-made ice cave carved beneath the Jungfraujoch plateau, a souvenir kiosk, a post office, a small summer skischool, husky dogs fighting each other and giving sleigh rides, and a 367-foot lift ride to a prominent observation terrace at the top of a small peak.

Ueli came to the dormitory the next morning. I had been expecting to bump into him soon because he divided his time between the Eiger Glacier Station Hotel and the Jungfraujoch Hotel. His speech was slow and careful, and all his movements had that same deliberate quality. He was strongly built, and the fact that he was balding at the front made him look even tougher. I suppose he was near forty years old at the time.

"Ah, Norman. I was not expecting you for a few days."

"I had a chance of a lift."

"I am busy now, but we must talk soon."

"Yes. There's no hurry. I'd like a few days to acclimatise."

Despite my eagerness to get on with the climbing, there was no sense in rushing into the headache, nausea and weakness which could result through attempting an exacting climb without being reasonably acclimatised. Four or five days would be enough to get reasonably used to the lower level of oxygen, one-third less at Jungfraujoch than at sea-level.

It was two days later that we had an opportunity to talk, in the restaurant.

"I think round about Tuesday it may be all right, if the weather is good," Ueli said. That was five days away. "On Tuesday there will be a good moon so we can start early. I will look for someone to go with us. I believe you should have two people with you. I think you may reach the summit in one day. Then we can come down and bivouac. Of course, we must wait for perfect weather."

He left for a few minutes, then came back and introduced a young, strong-looking man in his mid-twenties.

"This is Treas Schluneggar. He can go with us. So it is all settled, if the weather is good."

The days crept by, and hardly a cloud passed over Jungfraujoch without me glaring at it. On the whole the weather was good. Monday came, and at midday I began to pack my kit to take it by train down to the Eiger Glacier Station Hotel, from where we would start climbing the next day at about one a.m. Ueli came into the dormitory.

"I have just been on a rescue on the Eiger, on the west flank," he told me. "We had to bring down four people who were caught in a storm. I know them and they are good climbers. There is too much ice on the rocks at the top and it is very dangerous. I think we should not go now. Maybe if we have a week or two of good weather the west flank will be all right, but now it is too difficult. Even these good climbers had to be helped down. Luckily they were not hurt."

I had been expecting bad news because the weather did not look good, but all the same it was a great disappointment.

"I must go now, and we can talk later," Ueli said.

About four hours later, in the afternoon, I saw him again. He was wrapped in a duvet jacket and was on his way out of the hotel.

"I have to go to the Eiger again, to the west

flank. Someone has been killed. We are going by helicopter."

He hurried out. There was no doubt now that the conditions on the west flank were dangerous and would remain so for several days.

Next day Ueli told me about the rescue.

"An Englishman was killed and his three companions have been rescued. Conditions were terrible there. One of the men is in hospital in a very serious state. They were well equipped and I think they were good climbers."

Back at home Judy had heard a news broadcast which said that an Englishman had been killed on the west flank of the Eiger. She knew that I was about to climb and she couldn't help thinking that the dead man might be me. The announcer gave details of the accident, weather conditions, etc., while she listened. It was only at the end of the news item that the victim's name was given.

"Now we must decide what you will do," Ueli said.

"You think it will be a week or two before the west flank is in good condition?"

"Yes. Or perhaps more. It will take a long time for the ice to melt. You must decide

55

what you want to do. It will be a long wait. On the other hand, you could go and climb somewhere else. On the Matterhorn, for instance, where there is a high hut."

"I'd like to stay here."

"All right. Stay as my guest. One person more of less won't make any difference."

"I'd like to do some work in return. Washing dishes or something."

"You can wash some glasses, and if you do that you can eat and live with the staff."

That was very considerate of him, and work would help to pass the time. The routine of putting glasses through the glass-washing machine and drying them, slicing bread and washing spoons and dessert cups, kept me busy for about five hours a day. From the little room where I worked it was possible to keep watch through the restaurant windows on the weather. On the first day of work, Tuesday, it was misty, and on the Wednesday and Thursday too. Friday was dull and cloudy and so it went on. The peace of Tuesday evening was broken by thunderous crashes, and gigantic purple flashes illuminated the snowscape for miles around in a thunderstorm of frightening intensity. No wonder climbers who had been caught in lightning storms spoke of them in awe! The voice of thunder proclaimed that nature, not man, ruled these mountains.

The next day there was another snowstorm. Time dragged by. It was all mist and long faces. The weather improved a little over a few days.

"But we must still wait until conditions are very good," Ueli said. "We must be careful."

More glasses to wash, more bread to slice, more clouds to fill the sky, day after day. Wait, wait, wait. If only the Ogre of the Alps would drop his guard for a while! Improvements in the weather were short-lived. All I could do was wait. The only perseverance I needed had nothing to do with climbing but with waiting. It was simple—if I did not wait I would not have the chance to attempt the climb that year. Nearly four weeks went by, and I waited. Often it rained or snowed or hailed. I waited still. Then the weather began to improve, and was fine for long enough for hopes to rise. Was this the time, at last?

"We must talk to Treas," Ueli said one Monday. "If he is available we can go to the Eiger Glacier station soon. If he is not free I will find somebody else."

The weather remained good. Later that day I saw Ueli again.

"While the weather is good you must take the opportunity," he said. "I have seen Treas and he can go on Wednesday. Unfortunately I cannot go myself on that day, but Treas will find another guide. He will take my radio so he can get hold of Kleine Scheidegg in an emergency."

Treas and I sat in the restaurant to make plans the same day.

"We go to the Eiger Glacier station tomorrow," he said. "I will contact another guide to go with us."

"He will have to understand that we will need to bivouac."

"We will see. I have to go into the army the next day."

"We climb on Wednesday and you go into the army on Thursday?"

"Yes."

"But I can't get up and down in a day."

"We will see. Maybe you will go very fast and go up and down in a day."

"No. It will take me at least two days. It will be dangerous if I try to go too far in a day."

58

"Perhaps the other guide can stay with you."

He was evasive. I appreciated that Treas was approaching the venture cautiously and he couldn't be criticised for that. He did not, however, seem to be thinking far ahead.

"It's no good me rushing," I emphasised. "I can only do this if I take at least one and a half days and bivouac for one night."

"We will see what happens."

I weighed up the situation. It was possible that we could reach the top in a day and Treas could descend to the Eiger Glacier station while the other guide and I bivouacked. The two of us could then descend the next day. I wanted to pin down Treas and the other guide to more definite arrangements, but it turned out that there would be no opportunity to meet the other guide until an hour or two before beginning to climb. The plans were not satisfactory because they were indefinite, but they were not sufficiently vague to cause me to cancel the arrangements. We planned to start climbing shortly after midnight on Wednesday, August 25th.

On Tuesday I packed my equipment and went down by train to the Eiger Glacier Station Hotel. It turned misty during the afternoon and I doubted that we would climb. Another delay looked likely so I didn't feel very excited. Still, I went to bed very early in the evening in case the weather improved.

Treas woke me at two a.m. The sky was clear and starlit.

"We can go," he said.

I hurriedly put on my legs, hoisted up my rucksack and went to join Treas and the other guide, Robert, for breakfast. Robert was about the same age as Treas, in his mid-twenties. He didn't speak much English but anyway at that time of the morning we were silent mostly.

We sat around a coffee table in their hotel room and drank tea. Knowing that later I would be glad I had eaten, I forced down a few slices of bread and jam for energy. Occasionally Treas and Robert exchanged a few words in German. We were all still sleepy.

Fifteen or twenty minutes went by. Treas stood up and put a few odds and ends from my rucksack into his own. This reduced the weight I would carry. Good.

We pulled on warm outer clothing, slipped the rucksacks on and tramped to the front door of the hotel. The air outside didn't feel very cold. There was no wind and hardly any cloud in the sky.

"We put the rope on here in the light," Treas instructed, and we tied on to the rope with me in the middle and Robert at the rear. There were three or four yards of rope between Treas and me. Treas lit a candle lantern and Robert produced an electric torch.

"Ready?" Treas asked me.

"Yes."

So, here at last was a chance to see if I could get up the third of that great trio. It was nearing three o' clock. He led off up the rocky track which ran for a few yards beside the railway, then it went to the right of the tunnel. I found once more that walking in dark surroundings was difficult. People with feet can keep their balance in the dark partly because of leg and foot muscles which can tell them which way the ground is sloping and can also help to correct the balance. My feet told me nothing, so the eyes became more important for giving information about any alteration in the slope and nature of the land. My eyes could glimpse the stars, a few clouds and the dark, looming outline of the Eiger, but mostly they had to remain on the mobile patches of light cast on the uneven track by the candle lantern and the torch. In an hour or so it would get lighter and as the mountain steepened I would be able to use my hands as well—then there would be no balance problem.

The track continued along a moraine, the broken rubble which collects on the edge of a glacier. An avalanche crashed and rumbled down the mountain to our right, a long way away. The track came to natural steps of black rock which was wet and slippery. There were easy ways to choose through this section but it was not simple to pick the route in the dark: straying to the left or the right would have made the going much harder. Robert and Treas engaged in much discussion about the route as we picked our line up the rock, and now and then we retraced our steps to find an easier way.

"You wait there," Treas would say, going ahead a few paces. "OK. Come on now."

In daylight there would have been a fairly obvious route to follow. Slowly the mountain silhouettes took form, to become three dimensional as light fell on faces, snowfields, ridges. Eyes fixed on rock, on snow, on anything still, were like a long visual arm

62

stretched out to help balance. Wherever possible I kept both hands on the rock for steadiness and power. Sometimes when Treas and Robert walked upright it was better for me to scramble on all fours, like a chimpanzee, especially on the loose plates of rock which clinked like chunks of cast-iron as we walked over them. Within an hour of leaving the Eiger Glacier station, Treas extinguished the candle. The sky was light in the east, still dark in the west. The rock was just discernible, sloping on average at about forty degrees. There were a few steep steps of six to eight feet but the climbing was easy.

Lights glowed at the Eiger Glacier station and farther away pinpoints of yellow showed the village of Mürren. Treas talked with Robert but I remained silent, apart from breathing heavily. It was a serious occasion and the two men behaved accordingly; the Swiss of the Bernese Oberland could hardly be called light-hearted.

The Rotstock, a prominent pinnacle on the edge of the west flank, was to our left. It became lower than us, but looking across the mountain it was impossible to tell just when.

Half past four. The absence of cloud was encouraging. Thick mist masked the valleys but that was nothing to worry about.

We carried on over a long slope of small stones to the base of a snowfield which looked as if it had a gradient of about thirty degrees. Here was crampon territory, so we sat to strap the spikes on our boots. Treas, being in the lead on the rope, cut steps in the snow and ice to make it easier and safer. The ice was very hard in parts and required several strokes of the ice-axe to make a reasonable step, big enough to take nearly half a boot. Chop, chop, chop, chop. This was a restful period for me because there were a few seconds between each pace upwards. Plates and chips of ice slithered down as Treas chopped. The crampons bit reassuringly.

A beautiful pink glow spread over the white snows of the Jungfrau, backed by a sky of light blue. It was one of those superb moments that may suddenly strike the mountaineer as soon as he has a chance to take notice of his surroundings, when he reaches a summit and relaxes, or strolls on an easy path, or stops to put on an extra sweater. When there is time to look around, the mountains can in a moment remind you that just being amongst them is part of the fun. There may be a summit to aim for or a difficult face to climb, but you don't have to climb them. You can go to the mountains and walk or scramble or gaze. The choice is yours.

The snowfield was several hundred feet long and it took half an hour to climb. To get on to the cliff at the top of the snowfield we had to step across a gap where the frozen snow had separated from the cliff. Between the snow and the rock the gap could be seen stretching down for many feet. It was unlikely but possible that the top edge of the snow might crumble with a man's weight on it, so the rope was essential as we stepped across one at a time.

Treas crossed the gap in a nimble step and climbed to a place from which he could hold me if I popped down the hole. I reached the top edge of the snow, stood still on it and concentrated on keeping in balance before stepping over with the right foot. The crampon grated on a flat step of rock and I brought the left leg over to the cliff. Robert followed shortly after, and we continued up more rock as soon as our crampons were off. To the right the mountain was cut by a deep gully.

The limestone here was fairly steep and we

traversed to left and to right along ledges to choose the best route, rather than taking a direct line up the tiers. Treas gave me a pull on the rope in a spot where I was taking a long time. I prefer to climb without any assistance from the rope, but it was no time to be particular on such a long route. However, I have since changed my mind on that point, and I dislike being pulled on any route.

We climbed two or three hundred feet up and took another short rest. As we moved on we came upon verglas, a thin coating of ice making the rock look as if someone had attempted to preserve it under a layer of glass. There was no way to avoid the verglas so caution was needed with every move, whether when walking along a ledge or climbing upwards. I must have looked like a trainee tightrope walker, whereas Treas and Robert were able to move quite quickly and easily.

I was ever aware that mechanical failure of one of my legs was possible. If a foot dropped off I could still get down, and if a leg broke anywhere else I would use rope and an ice-axe to splint it. Descent would then be awkward but possible, even with the knee rigid.

How would I regard the climb if I had legs?

My viewpoint of any route was coloured very much by disability. I had embarked on a serious expedition and was four hours away from civilisation; the trip was not undertaken lightly. Yet a fit mountaineer could trot up to where I was in an hour and a half. He could have set out at the same time as me, climbed to the same height, returned to the Eiger Glacier Station Hotel and been in bed for an hour or more. For him, a bit of exercise before breakfast; for me, a journey which was exploring my limits. Anyone who is blasé about the danger on even the easiest of high mountain routes is either foolish or inexperienced, but the fact remains that the able-bodied man does not need to approach a route with quite the same serious consideration—he would not take two guides on the Eiger west flank, for instance.

We arrived at the Frühstückplatze, a level area of rock where climbers often stop to rest and eat, about two and a half thousand feet above the Eiger Glacier station. Less than three thousand feet of height to be gained. I felt fine. We sat down and looked across at the precipitous North Wall.

"I think you should not bivouac," Treas said. He pointed to the summit of the

Jungfrau. "See how the snow is blowing. The wind is too strong."

I had noticed the plume of wind-blown snow which streamed from the head of the Jungfrau. Obviously the wind was quite strong high up, even though the sun shone in a clear sky and we were in only a light wind.

"I have been on this mountain before and there is nowhere up there to bivouac," Treas added.

"People bivouac quite often on the west flank," I said. "In good weather and bad."

"It is not good with this wind. On the ridge up there we could be blown away," Treas said.

"We will not be on the summit ridge today," I pointed out.

Robert sat in silence. I wasn't sure that he understood what was going on.

I had climbed slowly but even so at the rate I was going we had a good chance of getting two-thirds of the way up the mountain in another two hours. Even though the climbing might be a little more difficult, I could keep up the same speed because we would not be climbing in the dark. In daylight and with plenty of time we could find a good bivouac site, I felt sure, and from two-thirds of the way up the mountain I should reach the summit the next day.

"We must not waste our lives," Treas remarked. "You have no feet and you don't want to lose your hands as well."

Cheeky monkey, I thought.

For several seconds I said nothing and stared at the rock at my feet. I was angry and extremely disappointed.

I considered going on alone but that would have been stupid. There was no alternative but to follow Treas's advice. Without companions the climb would have been too dangerous, and it was obvious that it was useless to argue with Treas. He had been reluctant from the start to talk about bivouacking, but if he was being over-cautious it was partly for my sake.

"We can go a bit higher so you can take some photographs of the North Wall," Treas said. "There is a good view from a bit farther up. Then we must go down."

Thanks for nothing, I thought.

How about going up farther and then saying I was too tired to descend? No, they would start to talk about a rescue party, or Robert could flatly refuse to go any higher the next day.

"Damn it! Damn it! Damn It!" I said in a murmur to myself. Disappointment tempered my anger, leaving only a slight feeling of annoyance. There was no point in making a fuss.

"If we're not going up to the top we might as well go down now," I said.

Treas took a radio from his rucksack and spoke into it to let someone at Kleine Scheidegg know that we were returning. A few words in acknowledgment came over the radio.

We started back down at once. All the way I was wondering if the next year I could find two good companions who would be prepared to bivouac on the Eiger. Also, I was thinking about the Matterhorn. The normal route is about the same length as the Eiger west flank. Part way up the Matterhorn is an emergency hut which could be used on the way up and down, so could it be that the local Zermatt guides would go with me? They wouldn't have to bivouac. It seemed preferable to try the Matterhorn rather than attempt to find two guides who would promise to bivouac on the Eiger. I could think of no other mountain with a hut so conveniently placed from my point of view.

A fifty franc note, worth about five pounds,

lay on the rock near where we climbed. I noticed it and picked it up, and a couple of minutes later two people floated through the nearby valley in the basket of a hot-air balloon. I stared at the note and the balloon for a long time to reassure myself that they were real.

As we approached the Eiger Glacier station Treas said, "It was good today. You are a strong man."

In the circumstances, such a statement gave me no pleasure. I felt drained of energy, not because of the effort but through disappointment.

From the hotel I rang Judy and promised to head for home so we could go on holiday together. We talked about going to Scotland to walk and climb. I felt that I was at a turning point where I could accept that the lengthy routes were too much for me, then I could spend my time on short and less exhausting routes. This feeling stayed with me for less than a day, until I was on the way back to England. Then I knew that I would continue to pursue long routes because failure was a bitter food. I would not be satisfied until I had climbed a few long routes or proved to myself that I could not manage them. If able-bodied mountaineers could tackle extremely hazardous routes involving several bivouacs then there was no reason why I should not bivouac on routes which were within my limits.

4

WITHIN minutes of arriving home I was persuading Judy that she would enjoy a mountain walking holiday in Switzerland. She liked the idea.

"Then I can try the Matterhorn," I explained. "There's a hut part way up so I wouldn't have to bivouac. Ueli thought it might suit me for that reason."

A week later we were in Switzerland. As soon as we reached Zermatt I went to the guides' office. The man in charge refused to find me a guide because he considered the climb to be too much for me.

Judy was waiting outside the office.

"Laughing boy in there says I might find a guide at the Hörnli hut, but I'm not very optimistic about finding one up there if he can't or won't find one in Zermatt."

Next I rang Felix Julen, the President of the guides, who was at the Hörnli hut at the time. It was from this hut that the Matterhorn was usually climbed.

"Well, come up to the Hörnli hut so a

73

guide can give you a test to see how you can manage. If you can climb all right two guides could go with you on the Matterhorn at the weekend or early next week."

The idea of a climbing test was sensible, and the suggestion meant that Felix Julen was at least prepared to give me a chance to show what I could do, rather than turning me down right away. It was good news but I was wary about letting my hopes rise too high.

We took a cable car to Schwarzee, 8,480 feet (2,582 metres), and then there was a rough trail to walk for a couple of hours to the Hörnli hut at 10,700 feet (3,260 metres). At first, the stony trail weaved up like any well-used path on a British moor or mountain. The final bit of track zig-zagged up the Hörnli Buttress to the hut. It was cold enough for small patches of ice and snow to remain there in the shadows. How many times we zigged and zagged, I don't know. Thirty, thirty-five, forty? The sharp turns to left and right went on and on, bringing us at last to the hut.

When I met Felix Julen he had changed his mind and suggested I should go to the guides' office again.

"The man there said he would not find a

guide," I explained. "You will remember, that is why I rang you. But there is plenty of rock around here for the test."

"Well, I think the weather may turn bad," Herr Julen said.

It did not, but it is not always easy to tell. However, impending bad weather was no reason for going down to the valley. There was rock to be climbed within a couple of hundred yards, and a hut and hotel to retreat to if the weather did turn bad. It was obvious that the embarrassed Felix Julen had had second thoughts, perhaps after talking with other guides. That a guide was cautious about climbing with me was understandable because I was an unfamiliar type of problem, but I was far from pleased that I had been invited up to the Hörnli hut for a test which did not take place.

"Poor thing. You haven't had much luck," Judy remarked later. "And it was his suggestion that you should come up here."

"If I met some other guides perhaps they would go. I don't know."

Felix Julen was well respected in the valley and on the mountains. Without his backing it was unlikely that I would find a guide. I felt like some kind of mountain leper.

"What will you do now, Norm?"

"Do you remember I told you about Eric Beard, the man who was killed while I was walking to Land's End?"

"The man the police thought was you?"

"Yes. Well, he wanted to climb Mont Blanc with me. He thought that as I couldn't go far in a day it would be a good idea to go hut to hut, doing a little bit at a time. There are three huts I can use on the way up. Might even miss one out on the way down."

"Fine. It's worth a try."

So we caught a train to Chamonix-Mont Blanc. The hyphenated name, linking the famous mountain with the town that thrives because of it, is officially used nowadays. Altitude: 3,400 feet. Population: about eight thousand people. A clean French mountain valley resort where dozens of hotels and restaurants await the tourist.

We booked in at a cheap dormitory and I went to the guides' office as soon as possible. There's just a chance, I told myself, that they'll help. Just a chance. I explained my circumstances and somewhat to my surprise the woman behind the counter said she would find me a guide, and asked me to return the following day.

An hour later Judy and I were having a meal in a café when two young Americans, a man and a woman, came in to eat. We got into conversation and they, Kevin and Barbara, said they hoped to climb Mont Blanc too. They were experienced rock climbers, and Kevin had some mountaineering experience, including having climbed Mont Blanc once before.

At the guides' office next day the woman didn't duck behind the counter or put on a false beard and glasses. She smiled and beckoned to a middle-aged man.

"Francis Bozon, Monsieur Croucher," she said.

The man and I shook hands. He was about five feet seven inches tall and strongly built. His dark hair, trimmed short, was turning grey at the back and the temples. He was serious looking, and obviously a quiet man. Chris Bonington has skied with him and once described him as a "good-tempered sheep dog". Even as we shook hands he was weighing me up. He spoke hardly any English so we struggled along in French.

"The lady has explained?" I asked.

"Yes."

"It may take me six days."

"I understand. You have climbed with crampons before?"

"Yes. Quite often."

"Where have you climbed?"

"Mönch, Jungfrau, some snow climbs in Britain, a little way up the Eiger west flank, rock climbing in many places for ten years. I've acclimatised for a month at eleven thousand feet."

"Have you a stove?"

"No."

"I have one. Gloves and something to cover the face?"

"Yes."

I didn't want to assume prematurely that he had made up his mind to go, but judging from his questions about equipment I was almost certain he had.

"When you buy the food, I would like plenty of soup and when you get the cheese, ask for *fromage de la montagne*. I like dried fruit too," Francis said.

No doubt at all. He would go.

"What's the weather like?" I asked.

"I think it will be all right tomorrow."

"I have bivouac equipment for the Vallot hut."

"There is an old observatory near the

78

Vallot hut. I will get the key and we can stay there. It will be more comfortable."

We wrote down a food list.

"I can't carry much weight," I explained.

"I will take all the food."

"That's good. It will help a lot."

"Have you a car?"

"No."

"We can use mine. We go along the valley and board a train at Le Fayet to Nid d'Aigle. Normally we would go from Les Houches but at this time of year the cable railway is closed. Tomorrow we'll walk from Nid d'Aigle to the Tête Rousse hut."

Judy could tell from the look on my face when I left the office that the arrangements had been made. She was waiting with Barbara and Kevin.

"We go tomorrow," I announced.

"Great!" Kevin said, and Judy beamed.

"I'd better go home. I've had twelve days of my holiday already and I want to save a few days so we can go climbing in Wales and Scotland."

"All right. Good job we have separate passports."

We all went for a meal. On the way Kevin explained that he was interested in my climbing because his father has an artificial leg.

Kevin and Barbara decided that they would not take the train up to Nid d'Aigle but would make the three-hour journey on foot from Chamonix, a trip which hardly any climbers bother with nowadays.

The sky was overcast when Judy and I got up the next day. We headed for the Co-op which was open by half past seven. We were hunting through the shelves for light food when Francis Bozon appeared and helped to fill the wire basket to the top with provisions before disappearing in a hurry. He had selected enough food for at least six days.

"He really does intend getting to the summit," Judy remarked. "I'm not judging just from the food, but from the way he behaves as well."

Judy and I had breakfast together, and after that things happened quickly. Francis Bozon arrived at the guides' office with his son, a cheerful young man who was training to be a pilot. Francis managed to pack all the food into his rucksack, Judy and I hastily made our farewells, and the trainee pilot attempted to get his car airborne on the road to Le Fayet. From Le Fayet the Tramway du Mont Blanc trundled up to the terminus at Nid d'Aigle

(7,800 feet) where we arrived at eleven thirty a.m. The sky was clear and the sun quite hot. We stepped from the train. Ahead of us, two and a half thousand feet to rise over an easy trail to the Tête Rousse hut.

I slipped my arms through the shoulder straps of my rucksack and fastened the waist strap to prevent it swinging around.

"I prefer that you walk in front," Francis said, indicating the rough path we would take southwards. I began to walk and could picture Francis watching each step, weighing up whether we should go on or not. With an ice-axe to steady me on boulders, I moved slowly and all the time watched where I was placing my boots. It became unpleasantly hot after a few minutes of exercise, but at least I didn't stumble. A bad performance at that stage could have meant the end of the whole trip.

Our route took us through rocky country, devoid of pretty colours but starkly impressive, where vegetation begins to give up the struggle to live. Not far above was the line where the snow remained all year round, and only a few species of hardy plants survived. We stepped over tough grass and small plants clinging where they could in the shelter of boulders and stones. No trees or bushes could live at that altitude. The view was far from exotically beautiful or lush, but was imposing and rugged. Here beauty was represented by wildness in simple form and limited colours.

Three minutes' walk brought us to a typical weaving mountain track, often turning sharply to the left and right, left and right, to gain height up a slope. The path was well used and the rocks faintly whitened and polished by countless boots.

Ahead, thirty French soldiers who had come up on the train drew away and in half an hour were out of sight. They were probably aiming to stay that night at the Aiguille du Goûter hut, which I wouldn't reach until the next day.

We passed a derelict hunter's cabin. The stone walls still stood but there was no roof. Perhaps it had been used by chamois hunters, from whom some of the guides are descended.

Words passed infrequently. Language difficulties restricted us a bit and I was concentraiting too much on walking to have time to chatter or take much notice of the scenery. On a popular hiking trail to Mont Blanc I was having to work hard where an able-bodied person could amble along. I would fare better where the mountain steepened.

My stumps felt slightly painful in much the same way as your feet may feel uncomfortable if you walk ten miles on a hot day. This unpleasant sensation would worsen until I stopped walking and climbing, but it would be a long time before it became distressing. There was cool mist only a few hundred feet higher up.

Odd patches of snow lay in dips in the ground and in the shade. We approached a huge rib of rock, part of the Aiguille du Goûter. The trail zig-zagged up in easy gradient over gritty mud at first, then over fractured brown rocks. The only noises were those we made, the sound of breathing, the scrape of an ice-axe, the crunch of a boot. As usual, I moved on all fours when the path sloped sufficiently to allow this. Thin mist came down around us and the air cooled. Turning now this way, now that, we followed the track. About an hour was enough to take us to the top of the rib, where we sat by the edge of the Tête Rousse glacier. From there on only steep rock would be free of snow and ice.

I knew we had to cross the glacier but I had no idea how far it was to the Tête Rousse hut.

We had taken just under two and a half hours. The guide-book mentioned that two and a half hours to three hours was a normal time from Nid d'Aigle to the Tête Rousse hut. It seemed reasonable to reckon that it would take me another hour to reach it.

"Five minutes to the hut," Francis said.

"Ah, good."

It was a surprise. Time spent at the Jungfraujoch had helped me to acclimatise well enough not to suffer from lack of oxygen. We were over ten thousand feet high and although the lower level of oxygen is not very serious at that height, one can rapidly become tired with exercise before acclimatisation.

There remained only two or three hundred yards to go, slightly upward, across the glacier. The mist rose and there was the wooden hut at 10,390 feet (3,167 metres). The snow covering the glacial ice was firm and no crevasses could be seen near us. We followed footprints which went towards the hut. A guide with a young lady client came down the glacier in our direction and stopped; they had come up on the same train. We shook hands all round and the guide explained that the young lady was suffering from altitude sickness. Once again I felt glad of that month at the Jungfraujoch. The guide chatted with Francis for a while before leading his client back towards the valley.

The Tête Rousse hut was not unlike a wooden army barrack hut. There was room for sixty people. The climbing season was drawing to a close, so the summertime guardian had departed. During the winter the hut would remain unlocked and there would be plenty of blankets for the few people who arrived.

Francis went outside to fetch a can of clean snow to melt, and he soon had some onion soup bubbling over a gas stove. He served it up and I made appreciative noises as I ate. Then I went outside and was sick. This was not unexpected as I had moved on all fours for quite a while, causing my stomach to be compressed. The altitude may have been affecting me too, but I didn't think so because I experience similar trouble when climbing stooped over at low altitude.

Kevin and Barbara arrived. They were tired after the trek from the valley. It was cold in the hut as there was no heating. We sat on benches with our elbows on wooden tables and talked as we sank mug after mug of tea, until the light began to fail. By then there were four other climbers in the hut. Everyone pottered about with torches, packing kit for an early start in the morning, and we all turned in by eight o'clock. The weather was good and Francis thought it would be fine the next day. Because of the cold we all wore plenty of clothes as we slept on the usual long, communal mattresses.

Under a blanket, I took my legs off, switched on a torch and examined my stumps. There was no damage on the left but the skin was rubbed away in two small patches on the right. If the slight injuries got worse they could prevent me climbing far, for when the flesh was badly damaged the stumps would swell and make movement very difficult. This had happened a few times on long walks; on the road it was possible (although unwise) to carry on walking until the muscles swelled and seized up. Going to such limits while climbing was not wise because of the lack of concentration brought about by prolonged pain. Already there was a very real threat to success. I washed the stumps in icy water, put antiseptic ointment on the injured spots, and went to sleep. I slept deeply at first but later in the night awoke for brief periods, to lie wondering if my stumps would manage the journey. Through a small gap between the window shutters the sky remained clear and starlit.

During one waking spell an alarm clock clattered unpleasantly. I looked at my watch—nearly half past five. It was still dark, and very cold. Francis stirred from the mattress a few feet away in the dark. He groped for his boots, put them on and clumped into the dining-room. The click of his cigarette lighter was followed instantly by the hiss of the gas stove.

The cold, rather than tiredness, kept the rest of us where we were, cocooned in blankets. After five minutes I sat up and punched the air to get warm. On with my legs, and I joined Francis in the dining-room. The room was faintly illuminated by the blue gas flame. He was making tea.

"The weather is good now," he said. "But the barometer has fallen a little." He knew this because he carried a small altimeter. If the altimeter reading crept up when we weren't climbing, the barometer was falling.

We drank tea and ate in silence. I finished a couple of slices of bread and butter. My stomach was settled and the stumps were not sore.

More people drifted in from the dormitory. Polythene bags rustled, buckles jingled, boots shuffled, karabiners (snaplinks) clacked together, crampons clinked as they were picked up. The sounds of preparation for a climb stood out starkly against the silence of the climbers. No one hurried. Gradually the sky lightened.

Francis finished eating and packed away the last of his equipment.

"You must take your time. Go at your own pace," he said.

"I hope I don't go too fast for you."

He laughed, appreciating the joke. He was not bad tempered but he didn't laugh often.

We carried our rucksacks outside and sat on the front step of the hut to strap on crampons. The light grey sky gave no hint of the way the weather would turn. The wind was light.

Francis passed me an end of the climbing rope and I tied it around my waist. Although it was not a dangerous glacier route, it was comforting to have the rope as a security measure while we crossed the edge of the Tête Rousse glacier.

A glacier grows in much the same way as an ordinary river, from precipitation which flows downhill. In the case of a glacier the snow which feeds it slides down slowly, almost imperceptibly: for instance, a large piece of rock borne by the Aletsch glacier in Switzerland took thirty-three years to move about four miles. There is another, more widely known example of how slowly a glacier moves: the body of an Englishman who disappeared on Mont Blanc after an accident was disgorged from the end of a glacier about four and a half miles from the scene of the tragedy, thirty-one years later. Cracks in the ice of a glacier may widen and deepen to form huge crevasses scores of feet deep. Crevasse openings are sometimes completely covered by snow, and when the snow is thick and frozen it can provide an easy passage. When warmed by the sun or warm air the snow may not support the weight of anyone who passes over. I was glad we were on a safe glacier.

Francis stepped forward, ahead by only a few yards. There were indistinct bootprints from the day before and we followed their line. The snow was firm but not crisp and icy, and sometimes under our boots it let out a squeal like a distant flock of geese or creaked with the noise of an old wooden chair. These sounds are so much a part of the scene that you might not notice that each of the many forms of snow has its own slight but definite sound under a boot.

The trail curved a little to the left, then to the right, in a steady pull upward over snow inclined at twenty degrees or less. We went up the left bank of the glacier; the words left and right are applied to a glacier as if you were looking at it from the source. We soon left the glacier behind and began to scale the Aiguille du Goûter, at the top of which our next proposed stopping point, the Aiguille du Goûter hut was visible. The hut stood 12,520 feet (3,817 metres) high at the top of a cliff. We had two thousand feet to climb up that cliff, via an easy rock rib. The angle of the rib, varying between thirty-five and fifty degrees, suited me because I could use my hands most of the time. The place is notorious for stonefall and several people have been killed or injured there. I was concentrating too much on where I was putting my boots to think much about falling stones, although my ears did pick up the sound of a few clattering down in the distance. The guide-book suggested up to three hours for this section from the Tête Rousse hut to the hut above, so I expected to take about four hours.

The rock was quite broken but offered plenty of safe holds. Parts to be taken with extra care were the many snow- and ice-covered rocks. We kept our crampons on all the time and alternately grated over rock or crunched across ice and snow. There were cracks which gave good holds, plus little natural steps of rock and small slabs so chipped and rough that hands or boots would grip anywhere.

"Wait here," Francis said at one point early on. He went ahead to a spot from which he could belay me across twenty feet of fairly steep snow and rock. He watched closely as I crossed. I was still being auditioned for the part.

The right stump hurt a little but the cold helped. The cliff faced west so was shaded from the early morning sun when it broke through the cloud.

The risk of stonefall would have been greater if there had been people above us to dislodge them, but apart from four figures descending far above there was no one to be seen. Francis kept a few paces ahead. I could see that he was picking the best places to stand in case I slipped. He remained silent and vigilant, always expecting the unexpected. At times he could walk up steps of rock where I had to climb, but it was pointless to envy him his powerful legs. If I had legs I would have to climb much more difficult routes to gain the same satisfaction as I would if I reached this summit . . . if, if, if.

About halfway up the rib we met the four descending climbers. Two were German and two were English. We exchanged greetings and they told us that conditions above the Aiguille du Goûter hut were good the day before. The men carried on down. I looked around at the sky, seeing that it was clear apart from a few slow-moving clouds high up. Not much wind, and that from the north. The signs were not bad, although the weather could change quickly. It could make the climb too dangerous for days on end and force us to turn back. And one fact I could not ignore: good weather for the length of time I needed was most unlikely. Two or three consecutive days of fine weather is common, but a week of continuous good weather is rare in the Alps. On the descent we could manage in moderately poor weather from the Tête Rousse hut to the Nid d'Aigle terminus, but above that we needed settled conditions.

At eight o'clock we stopped for a rest.

"This is a bad place to be after a storm," Francis remarked. "Ice covers the rocks. If the weather turned bad we would have to go down. But it looks good. Perhaps we can go as far as the Vallot observatory today if you feel all right. We must take advantage of the weather."

"Perhaps."

I didn't sound enthusiastic because the prospect of going from the Tête Rousse hut to the Vallot observatory (14,307 feet) in one day, missing out the Aiguille du Goûter hut, had seemed out of the question. The guide-book suggested it would take an able-bodied mountaineer six hours in reasonable conditions so it would take me at least eight hours, and possibly as many as ten hours. That was too long for the stumps if I wanted to continue to climb to the summit the next day. No, better to be prudent than too eager. Four hours to the Aiguille du Goûter hut would be a comfortable amount of climbing for one day. Caution could prevent me getting to the summit, but it would keep me out of trouble. After all, I was a learner.

I did not miss the significance of the proposal Francis had made: it meant that after watching me like a hawk he was satisfied that it was all right to aim for the summit.

We pressed on again. My boots gripped well on rough rock but it was the handholds which gave most reassurance. Below, we caught glimpses of two ascending climbers, probably Barbara and Kevin, who left the Tête Rousse hut a few minutes after our departure. Behind, we could look down into the green Chamonix valley and across to Switzerland. Geneva was there somewhere, not many miles away. Close by, in the same direction, were flat-topped mountains with distinct horizontal strata, high but free of snow, dry and barren. To our right was the Aiguille de Bionnassay, a nicely shaped satellite peak of Mont Blanc. The gently arched summit reaches close to thirteen thousand three hundred feet. Its north face, draped in a tracery of snow like an irregular net curtain, lay back from us a little. I was reminded of an account I read by one of two people caught on the summit of the Aiguille de Bionnassay in an electric storm. Lightning twice knocked them down and flashed so close that the writer's woollen balaclava helmet was singed. The pair were relieved and happy to get back to the Aiguille du Goûter hut after a difficult four-hour descent in bad weather. They realised just how lucky they had been when at the hut they learned that a young man had been killed by the same storm as he left the summit of Mont Blanc. He was struck by lightning. For the writer of that account the story was particularly upsetting because one of his friends had died in a storm at the summit of Mont Blanc a few years before. The day after their narrow escape the writer's companion decided to descend to the valley alone. He was killed, probably by stonefall, possibly by a slip, as he climbed down the way Francis and I were ascending.

By nine a.m. the hut perched on a ledge above us looked strangely close. If I needed four hours to get from the Tête Rousse hut to the Aiguille du Goûter hut, it would take an hour and a half to reach that ledge. Distances can be deceptive on mountains, but I was almost certain that the hut was only half an hour's climb away. Our pace remained constant and soon there was no doubt that the hut was close. In half an hour we were there.

It was a wooden building, covered in sheet metal outside. Some of the windows were round, like port-holes, and the long, low building looked like the hull of a stranded ship.

"Good. Three hours," Francis said, grinning. "Now you can rest and this afternoon we go on to the Vallot."

"I think so."

This was not what I had planned. What I had had in mind was to leave the Aiguille du Goûter hut only if the weather forecast was extremely favourable. I didn't mind being caught in that hut in bad weather, but the Vallot observatory was rather high to be stranded in. However, we had plenty of food and could stay warm in the observatory, so if the weather turned bad we could sit it out and descend at the first suitable opportunity.

Outside the hut we sat down to unstrap our crampons. In this hut, as in many alpine huts, it was usual to remove boots and stack them in racks in the entrance, and people wore rubber shoes provided by the hut guardian. Francis soon had his boots off and went in to order tea for us. I sat on a step and unlaced a boot, but when I came to slide it off it wouldn't budge. It was frozen to my metal

96

foot. After a good deal of time spent banging the foot on the ground, tapping the boot with my ice-axe and levering up the leather, I got one boot off. I was hard at work on the second one, thumping it with my ice-axe, when I looked up. A climber, walking past, was staring at me. I smiled at him and carried on with the job in hand. He moved away, open-mouthed. When I went into the hut I sat near him at a table. Giving me a funny look, he got up and went to a table at the far end of the hut. When you think about it, I don't suppose many people would want to sit close to someone who belts his feet with an ice-axe!

Inside the hut was room for about seventy people on the mattresses. The dining-room was large, like a village hall, and there were half a dozen other climbers there. Delicate Jack Frost leaves decorated the windows but it was warm inside the building. We sat at a table and drank tea from large bowls. Our talk centred at first around the weather.

"It may change soon," Francis explained. "The barometer is still falling."

"The wind looks strong above here now." This was clear from the streamers of snow being blown from crests.

"It is, but not too strong for us to go on. I

have spoken to the guardian and we can rest here now."

"That's good."

"And at midday we start for the Vallot?"

It was a question, not a statement.

"Yes."

We had reached the Aiguille du Goûter hut much more quickly than I had expected. I'd had enough failure for that season and was in no frame of mind to lose an opportunity.

"We will rest then, for two hours," Francis said.

We made our way to a dormitory where I took my legs off. The right stump was bleeding from the end, where the bone finished. The wound was no bigger than a 2p piece but the small area of damage was surrounded by swollen flesh. I was tempted to stay at the hut until the next day.

Two hours of dozing sped by. Back in the dining-room we had a bowl of soup each. Kevin and Barbara were there, having arrived about an hour after us. Barbara was not used to climbing on ice and snow-covered rock, so they decided that their four-hour stint up to the Aiguille du Goûter hut was enough for a day.

"See you tomorrow at the summit," Kevin

said as Francis and I prepared to leave.

Boots on, crampons strapped under boots, glacier cream and lip salve smeared over skin, goggles on, rope tied, gloves on. This was the first time we required glacier cream and lip salve to protect the skin from harmful ultra-violet rays. Without goggles, the dazzling sunlight reflected from the snow could be unpleasantly bright and could even cause snow blindness. Crevasse danger was small the way we were going. The hut guardian provided a spare ice-axe to help me along. It would be snow and ice all the way from the Aiguille du Goûter hut at 12,520 feet (3,817 metres) to the Vallot observatory at 14,307 feet (4,362 metres) and from there to the summit.

It was one o'clock when we started. In some mountain areas it would have been unwise to leave so late, but on this part of the route there were no stonefall hazards, dangerous crevasses were rare, and avalanches were unlikely.

The sun beat down on us as we mounted a fairly steep snow slope, which rose for a hundred feet behind the Aiguille du Goûter hut. We turned to follow the ridge at the top of the slope towards the south, tending soon southeastwards. On the right side the rocks of the Aiguille du Goûter fell away steeply—two thousand feet of cliff is quite a sight when you walk along the top. A well-trodden trail led across the ridge, which was an extended mound of snow like a huge long-barrow curving along the clifftop. It was a spectacular, yet not dangerous, place to be.

Our boots sank perhaps five or six inches in the snow. I walked in Francis's footprints because his weight had compacted the snow there. While sorting out equipment and rejecting all but the essential articles, I had decided against taking ski-baskets for the ends of the ice-axes. I soon regretted leaving them behind, for the ungainly craft needed outriggers on soft snow. With great effort, muscles were forced to correct balance; two ice-axes with ski-baskets could have done the same job with almost no effort.

As we gained height across a gently rising snowfield the wind grew stronger. Around us, the elements had sculpted smooth, soft undulations, and only rarely was the glistening snow scarred by a broken cliff of ice or a dark crevasse.

Francis watched the colour and texture of the snow. Any which glistened with a crust of ice was firmer than the whitest areas. Darker patches in shadow, where the wind blew and the sun didn't cast its warmth, were harder too. Sometimes he could see places where powdery snow was being whipped up by the wind and he would avoid them. The character of the mountain's white mantel could be read from its complexion and it changed every few feet.

An hour passed and I began to find it hard going. The right stump hurt a lot. I struggled to inhale sufficient oxygen to fuel a straining body. The gradual incline, fifteen to twenty degrees, dragged on and on up the snow: a hundred yards, two hundred yards, three hundred yards, five hundred, eight hundred. My ice-axes sank alternately in the snow to the left and right and provided hardly any support. Our boots, after being raised clear of the snow, would be thrust forward to sink six inches, six inches through which they had to be raised at the next step. How much worse it would be at twenty-five thousand feet in the Himalayas and on powder snow, I thought, and at the same time I cursed myself for venturing out on soft snow. We ploughed on.

Two hours after leaving the hut I was very tired.

"I must rest," I called out to Francis.

"All right."

Dropping slowly to my knees, I stayed where I was, kneeling. It was as relaxed a position as any other in the circumstances.

"We are going slowly," Francis remarked.

"Yes, but Vallot today," I said between gasps, "and perhaps the summit tomorrow."

"Perhaps."

By three o'clock the sun was much less hot than when we left the hut. The biting wind precluded an extended rest and in two or three minutes we toiled on. The gradient lessened, for we were nearing the top of a huge dome of snow, the Dôme du Goûter, a hump with a width of about seven hundred yards. Gradually, almost imperceptibly, the snow levelled out and became firmer. Though bathed in sunlight, the snow was frozen by the wind racing across it. We trudged over the top of the Dôme. It had taken over two and a half hours from the hut by the time we reached the top of the Dôme. The summit of Mont Blanc was only a mile and a half away. Hemmed in by dozens of summits of over ten thousand feet, Mont Blanc does not dominate the scene from all viewpoints, particularly from the valleys. Seen from the Dôme du Goûter none of the surrounding peaks could challenge its superior height.

I wondered if twenty-four hours later I would look on the summit with contentment and satisfaction, or with disappointment. Hope was so strong that it was uncomfortable.

The Vallot hut and observatory, half a mile away, came into sight. To reach the observatory it was plain to see that we had to descend from the top of the Dôme du Goûter to a saddle called the Col du Dôme, and from there climb a slope of snow and ice at about thirty-five degrees. Had I been fresh it would have been easy, but I was struggling to keep going.

On the descent of the Dôme the sun no longer shone. Whether this was because it was behind the Dôme du Goûter or clouded over I did not notice, but the air turned bitterly cold. Without the warming rays of the sun the wind could have chilled the body and sapped the strength to a dangerous extreme in a short time. I was glad there was not far to go. It was like being forced to run for hours on end: I would have been relieved to have stopped at any moment. There was no chance of any more than a brief halt, though, until we reached the hut, because it would have been unwise to have lingered for long in that wind.

Icicles formed on my beard and my gloves froze stiff. The cold affected me more than usual because of the fatigue brought on by between six and seven hours of climbing.

Despite the freezing wind, I had to stop to catch my breath when we reached the Col du Dôme. It was there that I noticed that my fingers were numb.

The wind buffeted from the left side in gusts which made it difficult to keep balance. It was like walking in a crowd with people shoving you around. I felt close to exhaustion as we began the two or three hundred yard climb up to the observatory. Normally it would have taken about ten minutes but I was stopping every fifty yards to catch my breath. Each time we halted Francis stood a few feet above me and now and then I thought he looked a bit concerned. I hoped he was not deciding that we should go down the next day. Had I made a mistake in going from the Tête Rousse hut to the Vallot observatory in one day? It was twice as far as I had planned for that day. Should I have stuck to my original plan? I wasn't sure.

The rasp of crampons on ice, the slightly

wheezing hiss of our breathing and the rush of the wind filled the air. Little by little we went on. I could feel my crampons bite; I don't know how I can tell that the crampons are firm but I do know when they are. The wind was blowing snow away in whirling white clouds to expose more ice. Though working very hard, I was cold.

At last we reached the observatory, a wooden hut built in 1890 on a tiny isolated outcrop or rock. The hut was about twenty-five feet long and ten feet wide, and the windows overlooked the Dôme du Goûter. A few yards away was the Vallot emergency hut, a life saver in bad weather. We were using the observatory because there was a big stove and wood there, and it was more comfortable. I wondered how many scores of wearying treks had been made to take the hut timbers there piece by piece.

Francis produced a key and unlocked the door. We took off our crampons and went in. There were a couple of tables and two chairs, rows of shelves along the walls and two beds with blankets piled on them. The shelves were crammed with pots, pans and crockery. A small stove stood near the door. The place had an atmosphere of passing time: enamel pans stacked by plastic bowls, candles and new electric torches, polaroid sunglasses on a shelf near some seaside postcards which were forty or more years old, and Francis's portable gas stove on a table above a box of firewood.

"How are you now?" Francis asked.

"Tired and a bit ill, but happy."

"You have climbed for seven hours today. That is quite a lot at this altitude."

"Yes. I don't like soft snow. I made a mistake not bringing ski-baskets to fix on the ice-axes."

"Four hours is a long time from the Aiguille du Goûter hut to here."

"Much too long," I agreed.

Francis soon had the stove going and we drank soup and tea. Icicles from my beard plopped into the tea as I sipped. The sky grew dim and we lit a candle. The hut groaned and shook with the force of the wind which roared outside. Even with the fire blazing it was quite cold, so we sat close to the stove.

"The wind is bad," Francis remarked. "If it stays like this we will not be able to go up. We may have to go down."

We turned in early, each wrapped in a huge pile of blankets. My right stump was swollen

106

and bruised and blood had caked at the end. If we continued to climb the next day it would get worse. The normal time from the observatory to the summit was about two hours. If the weather was good the next day the only thing to do would be to carry on. It wasn't working out at all like the reasonably easy, injury-free trip I had had in mind. I was learning about my limits the hard way.

The wind howled and tugged at the hut all night. The building creaked and shuddered. By four a.m. it had not eased, nor at six o'clock, nor seven. Francis got up and lit the fire. He stood for a while at the window. From my heap of blankets I called out; I knew the answer already.

"Can we climb?"

"No. The wind is too strong."

I settled back and fell asleep again, to be woken a few minutes later by Francis with a cup of tea. I drank the tea, then with a feeling of dread reached for my legs and put them on. It would be obvious right away if the overnight rest had been enough, I told myself, as I stood up. My heart sank. The stump was still very swollen and tender, in which case further movement would increase the damage rapidly. If the weather cleared up, which was unlikely, there would be a painful journey ahead.

Outside, the sun was shining but white whirlwinds of snow scurrying across the Col du Dôme were further evidence of the raging wind.

We drank soup and ate ham and bread. Francis hated being inactive and wandered around like a caged animal. On the other hand I sat as much as I could. I hoped he didn't realise that this was because I found it painful to stand. He made no complaint when left to do all the odd jobs.

There was no feeling in the ends of my fingers. The skin on the tips was strangely hard, and when I pressed them flat on the table they took a long time to return to their proper rounded shape. I avoided mentioning to Francis that my fingers were very mildly frostbitten because I was afraid news of that kind might have tipped the scales in favour of us retreating. He might have been annoyed about my carelessness in not putting on another pair of dry gloves. It was not serious but it taught me a lesson.

At about half past five that same morning Kevin and Barbara set out to try to get to the summit from the Aiguille du Goûter hut. Six more people left the hut at the same time. The wind was so strong that two people soon headed back. Before long, two more returned to the hut. Kevin and Barbara kept going as far as the Vallot hut and observatory, where they came to the conclusion that it would be silly to go any farther. A short distance ahead of them two German brothers had a disagreement about whether they should continue. One detached himself from the rope and walked towards the top. The way to the summit was clearly visible, as were the huge streamers of snow being torn from the summit ridge by the wind. The other brother, and Kevin and Barbara when they arrived at the hut, watched and waited. The longer they sheltered in the hut, the more they became convinced that Francis and I had headed for the summit and come to grief. What they didn't know was that they were in the emergency hut while we were safe close by in the observatory.

The lone German eventually reached the summit and began the descent. His luck held, and he rejoined his brother. Together they started back to the Aiguille du Goûter hut, followed closely by the two Americans.

At about half past ten Francis noticed

someone descending the slope near the observatory and we went out to watch them.

Barbara and Kevin waved excitedly when they saw us.

"We thought you were dead!" Kevin bawled above the noise of the wind.

"No. Not by a long way," I called back.

"You going to try tomorrow?" he wanted to know.

"If the weather's all right. You be coming back tomorrow?"

"No. We've had enough today. We're frozen. But good luck to you."

"Thanks. See you in the valley."

Kevin and Barbara carefully cramponed down the icy slope. For some reason the German who reached the summit had taken off his crampons, so it was not surprising that he slipped, dragging his brother behind him down the slope. They slithered, gaining speed, until they were able to halt their slide with ice-axes. Kevin told me later that the one who had reached the summit was not very alert on the way back to the Aiguille du Goûter, and he almost stepped into a crevasse. The climb had drained him to the stage where he could not think or act properly.

The wind blustered all day, hustling up

flurries of snow. We drank tea and kept the fire going, read a two-week-old French newspaper from end to end, and talked within the limits of my French about Francis's teaching job with the National School of Ski and Alpinism at Chamonix. He had won many ski competitions when he was younger.

Francis stood looking out of the window for long periods or paced the room. At three o'clock he was standing at the window when he said, "I think it is finished for you."

Probably true, I thought, but I hated to hear the words.

"It's in the hands of God now," I said. I couldn't decide whether God would be interested in getting anyone up a mountain. Despite the misery I felt, I tried to remain outwardly optimistic so we would not make definite plans to descend the next day.

"It would be bad to be caught here in a storm," Francis said. "We could be stranded for days. Tomorrow, probably we should go down."

"How's the altimeter?"

"It's dropping."

"That's good."

"Perhaps."

Success hung by a thread, a thin, thin

thread. The chance of reaching the summit could fall away and be lost. Even the descent could be difficult if snow conditions were bad; in such conditions the route was dangerous and tiring, the guide-book said.

In the late afternoon the sun began to sink into a hummocked sea of clouds above which only a few of the highest mountains, including the one we were on, peeked out. The red sun, big and round, slid from a sky of gold and yellow into the cloud in a display which in itself might have made the journey to the observatory worthwhile for a mountaineer who had no summit ambitions.

"The sun was watery when it went down," Francis said. "It's a pity."

We lit a candle and had more soup, tea, cheese, bread, ham and dried fruit. The wind hammered away at the observatory. There was none of the usual excitement and preparation in anticipation of a day's climbing: we just went to bed and fell asleep.

"You might manage Mont Blanc," Eric Beard had told me in 1969.

"You think so?"

"Well, if you find it's too much you'll have to turn back. Keep that in mind and you'll be all right. Have you got anyone to go with you?"

"No."

"I'd like to go. Should be an interesting trip. I'll see if John Cleare can go too."

John Cleare is a well-known mountaineer and photographer. After Eric's death I wrote to John and asked him for advice on how he thought I should tackle the route. That dismal night in the Vallot hut, passages of John's letter came back to me. He wrote:

Below the Vallot hut, the last one before the top, it is possibly easier by the Mulets and Grand Plateau as opposed to the Tête Rousse and Goûter huts, but it is one long haul rather than two, and there are icefall and crevasse problems which I would think you would find more awkward . . . for instance leaping a crevasse . . . than the steep scramble over rock up to the Goûter hut. All taken into consideration you have chosen the best route.

Mont Blanc is a very big mountain. By the route we are discussing, it is easy in good conditions. But it's nearly 16,000 feet high, and even without the altitude the distances involved are great. Like all big mountains it is very dangerous, weather changes abruptly and in bad weather even the easy route has killed many experienced mountaineers. If you do it in fine weather you think of it afterwards as a doddle—but in storm the summit plateau is perhaps the worst place to find the way off in the whole alps. You'll need five days perhaps of settled conditions which in some years is fairly rare, although on the way down you might make two stages in one go.

It is a serious business, but provided always that you take the correct precautions and have the right gear and don't wind your neck out you'll have no difficulty. On mountains discretion is always the better part of valour. No one laughs at you for turning back before the storm, though they curse when they have to collect the victims after the storm.

It's certainly been a tragic few months. Another friend of mine, and of Beardie's it happens, was killed last weekend on Ben Nevis in that avalanche. It will take a lot of getting used to not having either of them around any more.

Still, let's get you up Mont Blanc. Life must go on, they'd want it that way.

A number of times during the night I woke up. The wind continued unabated. Forlorn thoughts seem worse at night and I was glad to spend most of the time in sleep rather than thought.

I didn't see the dawn break. In the early daylight I looked at my watch. Half past six. It was cold and quiet in the building. There was no noise. No noise at all. Then I realised why: no wind! The wind had died down!

Francis started to shuffle about. He looked at his watch too, then sprang out of bed. Hurriedly pulling on his boots, he called out to me at the same time.

"The wind has gone! We can climb!"

It was evident as soon as I stood that thirty-six hours of rest had reduced the swelling on the right stump. The pain was slight.

We gulped down tea and gobbled bread and ham before packing a minimum of equipment into our rucksacks.

Outside the observatory we put on our crampons. Francis locked the hut. It took only seconds to rope up. It was about seven o'clock. The sun was bright in a clear sky. There was hardly any wind. Two hours to the summit, the guide-book said. In two and a half hours, I thought, I could be on that summit. What if the weather turned bad, forcing us to retreat? That would be extremely unlikely in such a short time. Stonefall? No danger. Avalanches and crevasses? Hardly any risk at all. Mechanical failure of legs? A bare possibility. A fall? I could be confident that if I slipped Francis would soon have the rope tight. An awkward landing after a short fall was probably the greatest potential hazard.

"O.K.?" Francis asked.

"Yes."

"Then we will go."

He led the way. The wind had stripped the slope behind the observatory of much of its snow. We cramponed upwards across ice and hard snow for a few yards, then swung along, left, right, left, right, at a smart pace up a gradually rising snowfield.

Four people, in two parties, were ahead of us by two or three hundred yards. They had started out early from the Aiguille du Goûter hut. We could see no one below.

The slope narrowed, became steeper and joined the Bosses ridge. Apart from the difference in colour it looked like a desert sand-dune. We charged along the crest. I breathed like a stag pursued by hounds, and Francis coughed frequently.

The pace didn't slacken across two snow

humps, the Grand Bosse and the Petite Bosse. The top of the Petite Bosse is less than a thousand feet below the summit. A few feet to the right was the border with Italy; we may have walked right on the border in some places.

My fingers were still without feeling in the ends, but holding two ice-axes was no problem.

The route descended into a slight dip after the Petite Bosse. Two of the other climbers were only twenty or thirty yards ahead, and the other pair were not far in front of them. We were not racing, but it was clear that two nights spent above fourteen thousand feet had aided acclimatisation.

"Rest for a minute, please, Francis."

"All right."

The observatory was already an hour's march away behind us. Time had flown. The weather showed no sign of changing.

I caught my breath and we began the trudge up snow past some rocks, called the Rochers de la Tournette. That left four hundred feet to rise. The ridge to the summit stood out unmistakably. From a broad slope it grew up at an easy angle to the top of the mountain. This was the most exposed place above the observatory: the top of the ridge narrowed until it was about as wide as two bootprints, side by side.

On the broader section of the ridge, low down, we kept up a good speed. The two men in front decided to belay right away. Whenever one of them moved forward the other stood still with the rope passed around an ice-axe which was rammed deep into the snow. The theory is that if someone falls the ice-axe will remain in the snow as an anchor; snow conditions are rarely suitable for holding more than a very short fall. Francis considered that we did not need to belay on the lower part of the ridge so we tramped past the two men by walking below them on the slope to our left.

"The suffering is almost over," the leader of the pair said jokingly to us in French.

Soon after, Francis went seventy or eighty feet ahead while I remained stationary. As soon as he had his ice-axe firmly implanted in the snow and the rope around it, he called for me to advance. When I reached him he moved ahead again on his own. Four or five times he belayed in this way. The pair a few yards in front, two Italians, were belaying as well. They belayed several times, then they just walked on because the ridge broadened. We followed them, a few yards behind. They stopped, took off their rucksacks and started taking photographs. They were at the summit. Within seconds we were beside them, 15,781 feet (4,807 metres) high on the top of Mont Blanc.

Francis and I shook hands.

"Thank you," I said. "You have been a patient guide."

Weeks and months of tensions simply disappeared, as if washed away. I was ecstatic just to be there, without fully knowing why I had gone. But wow, I was there! There was a sensation of excitement, as if I felt good music without hearing any. Sometimes a glimmer of that summit feeling comes back at an odd moment and I know again why I went. The ascent, once over, never dies.

The date, September 18th, 1971, was exactly two years after I walked out of John o' Groats.

The settled weather allowed a good view across the Pennine Alps, to the Matterhorn and Monte Rosa. Between them and Mont Blanc stood mile after mile of snowy peaks, a gigantic mountaineers' playground. I hoped to explore it all one day.

We had taken an hour and three-quarters from the observatory to the summit. After about fifteen minutes we were on the way down, this time with me in front.

Back at the observatory, Francis started to peer at the sky again.

"Now we can rest, but we ought to go down to the Aiguille du Goûter hut this afternoon. This would not be a good place to be stranded."

The descent continued. An hour from the observatory a party of three alpinists overtook us. They had climbed Mont Blanc by a different route. Francis chatted to their leader, who patted me on the back and said "Bravo!" before moving on.

"A guide?" I asked Francis.

"Desmaison."

"René Desmaison?"

"Yes."

"He is well-known in Britain."

"He is well-known wherever people climb."

Desmaison is a tough and controversial climber. In February 1971 he was at the centre of an alpine drama when, with another guide called Serge Gousseault, he was stranded in a storm on an extremely hard climb. Gousseault perished slowly after they had spent days without food in cruel winter conditions at high altitude. Desmaison was rescued by helicopter. Criticisms of his judgment and conduct flew about, pros and cons were weighed, hotly disputed and never settled. It is a pity that the incident cast such a shadow over the career of a brilliant alpinist who has made some outstanding ascents.

Francis and I watched as Desmaison and his two companions charged quickly out of sight. We continued slowly over the soft snow. My right stump became swollen and painful again. If only I had stopped at the Aiguille du Goûter hut on the way up, instead of pressing on to the observatory, the stump would have been all right. But if I had stopped at that hut Francis might have decided against heading for the observatory in high winds the next day. We might not have reached the summit at all. No, the discomfort was a small price to pay.

The descent was not easy for Francis as my snail's pace prevented him taking rhythmic strides. For the first time he became impatient and his voice sharp.

"No, move to your right! The snow is firmer there!" he barked. Even a good-tempered sheep dog may snap now and then.

121

Few people could have remained patient when fatigue made my movements progressively more slow and sloppy. On top of that, he had risked his reputation as a guide by accompanying a disabled person. If any mishap had occurred on the mountain he would have been criticised heavily. He was entitled to be a bit agitated.

We took three and a half hours to struggle from the Vallot observatory to the Aiguille du Goûter hut. An able-bodied party could have managed in half the time. The slushy snow yielded underfoot and occasionally we sank almost up to our knees. Once more I learned that it was all I could do to keep going in such warm conditions on snow. Nowadays I could manage but I had to go through experiences like this to learn to cope.

At the Aiguille du Goûter hut I went straight to the dormitory and flopped on a bunk. As soon as I lay down I was seized with violent coughing fits. My overworked back muscles felt as if I'd been carrying a cow around all day, the nausea came on again, the right stump was in very poor shape, my fingers were still dead (they were back to normal in a week or ten days), my head ached with a pulsing pain, I shivered and my nose started to bleed. Did I still feel it had been worth it? Without a doubt.

I slept deeply and the next day we flew down from the hut by helicopter taxi. Really I wanted to climb down but one stump needed a day's rest, a day which Francis did not wish to waste in inactivity. He was afraid that the weather would turn bad and leave us stranded in the hut for days and cause him to lose lucrative guiding time. I suggested that if he wanted to go down I would find someone to descend with the next day, or whenever the weather allowed, but he would not hear of this. In fact we argued for some time for I felt that while it was stupid to damage the stump further, flying was taking too easy a course. It was appropriate to my circumstances to make good use of the hut. It seems strange, looking back, because the stumps would take three times as much punishment nowadays. But these were early days and I was still finding out how the leg amputee could best manage in the mountains. With mixed feelings I agreed to fly, rather than to climb, but there were two temptations: the chance of my first helicopter ride was difficult to resist, and the fare was less than I would have paid in guide fees.

The Aiguille du Goûter hut was frequently visited by helicopter and there was a rather precarious landing pad nearby. On a sharp snow ridge the pad had been levelled out at the top, at the apex of the sloping sides. The helicopter had to alight on a flat snow area about the size of the floor of a large room.

We sat on the edge of the landing pad with our heads down. The Alouette III helicopter hovered over and dropped with a screaming racket and tremendous downdraft. We had read in an old newspaper at the Vallot observatory that a helicopter had crashed in the same place two weeks before. Crouched low as we were, the big rotor blades were high above, but the tail rotor looked close and menacing, likely to turn us to mincemeat in an instant. The aircraft settled gently and we scrambled in. In front, the cliff of the Aiguille du Goûter dropped two thousand feet. The helicopter lifted a little, tilted forward and plunged down the cliff. For a couple of seconds I couldn't be sure whether we would crash or not, then we were floating forward and down, away from the cliff. The pilot made a gradual descent so our ears had time to get accustomed to the change in altitude. We hung over the sunny valley which, from ten thousand feet, appeared like a pretty relief map of itself. Tiny houses lay clustered along thin, twisting ribbon roads; fields were irregular patches of green fitted into a carpet for the valley floor; it might have been green baize stretched up the valley walls except that as you got closer the individual trees could be picked out; the rock formations above the tree line might have been moulded in plaster and painted brown, and the snow on top had been left unpainted.

The helicopter passed low over Chamonix, went farther up the valley, skimmed over some trees and landed on a tarmac area amongst them. There was an ambulance waiting. I don't know what message had reached the driver, but it had gone wrong somewhere. As Francis and I alighted from the aircraft the ambulance driver ran his eyes over us and a rather sickly smile crossed his lips as if to say, "Someone's got it wrong again."

There was a complaint in a French newspaper about an abuse of the helicopter service—it turned out that the helicopter I flew in was supposed to function only in emergencies. I was pleased that the complaint was made because it showed that everyone knew that the ride had not been imperative. However, I was disappointed that it had not been pointed out to me that the normal commercial taxi was not available at the time. Had I known that I would have climbed down the next day, or whenever the weather was good. As it turned out, the weather was good the next day.

The experience made me sure of one thing: I would never again descend by helicopter taxi.

The next morning the guides presented me with a certificate, signed by the chief guide and Francis. A few reporters came to the guides' office and I made a radio recording in hesitant, inaccurate French. Even one of the most graceful languages in the world sounds as if it's wearing hob-nailed boots when spoken with a Cornish accent. Francis was recorded too, and although I didn't understand all that he said I was pleased to hear some of his comments.

"We took about four hours from the Vallot to the summit and back. That is good time," he said. "And he walks better on crampons than many normal people."

A short celebration with some guides was followed by lunch with a press photographer, his pretty girlfriend and two young guides who had completed an extremely hard ascent.

That same day I flew home from Geneva. Perhaps it was really September but I was a little boy, it was Christmas and Mont Blanc was mine.

5

LIFE was busy after Mont Blanc. Following a few television and radio broadcasts I was picked as one of the thirteen "Men of the Year" who attended a luncheon at the Savoy Hotel in London. It was interesting to meet the other "Men of the Year": the world motor-racing champion, Jackie Stewart; the English cricket captain, Ray Illingworth; John Dawes, who captained the British Lions rugby team; Sir Geoffrey Jackson, the former British Ambassador in Montevideo who spent months as a prisoner of guerillas; Chay Blyth, the solo round-the-world yachtsman; Jack Bodell, the boxer. As well as these famous personalities a soldier, a policeman, an R.A.F. pilot, a lifeboat coxswain, a fireman and a submarine captain were presented with certificates for bravery or achievement. It was sobering to meet men who accepted danger as a part of jobs they felt they ought to do. The sportsmen may have looked more dashing but we were humbled by the presence of men who risked their lives for others.

The Eiger was on my mind so I kept in training by climbing and walking. All the time I hoped to meet two or three good climbers who would leap at the chance of going up the west flank of the Eiger, but no one turned up.

In September 1971, Georges Nominé, one of France's top climbers, offered to do the route with me in the summer of 1972. I appreciated his offer but hoped that I would not need to hire a professional like Georges. I had served my apprenticeship with a number of guides and felt it was time to branch out. Sadly, in March 1972 Georges was killed in a mountain accident when he fell a long way from the top of a very difficult climb.

At the annual dinner of the South Wales Mountaineering Club, in February 1972, I made a point of outlining my intention to climb the west flank. A few people showed interest, and most of them were amongst the best dozen mountaineers in the club. They all asked for time to think about the climb before deciding whether or not to accompany me.

The tedious wait for good conditions on the west flank in 1971 was engrained in my mind; for this reason I made sure I would be free to climb for several weeks in the summer. Mountaineering dictated my life pattern, and I took a temporary job. The job lasted until midsummer, which meant I would be free to spend as long as I could afford in the Alps then. It may seem irresponsible to count mountaineering before a career, but I thought ahead to the day when I would be fifty or sixty years old. Lets say I looked back and realised I could possibly have climbed the Eiger but did not do so because I chose regular pay or job security instead. How much would I regret not having made the climb? A great deal, I'm sure. Age, family responsibilities, a minor permanent injury to hip or back, lack of money or short holidays—each could rob me of the Eiger ascent if I delayed too long. Thirty-one is not old for a mountaineer, but as the years creep by opportunity can suddenly or slowly disappear, if you don't take it when the time is ripe. Also, I had no intention of getting in a rut until it seemed inviting.

At the Roehampton limb centre my fitter, Brian Campbell, suggested strengthening the artificial legs and the work was soon carried out. This reduced the possibility of mechanical failure from the stresses of mountaineering.

A one-legged man told me one day how much relief he found from wearing a very thin nylon sock to protect the stump from abrasion. I rang the limb centre to enquire about nylon socks and some were forwarded to me at once. The increase in the punishment the stumps could take was noticeable immediately. At the time I did not realise just how much those socks would benefit me.

Shortly after the annual dinner of the South Wales Mountaineering Club I met some of the members again, at a party. One of them, Dave Parsons, was keen on the Eiger west flank plan. He grasped the full implications of climbing within my personal limits: he realised that to force myself up a mountain and all the way back to a valley as quickly as possible would often be more dangerous than going at a comparatively leisurely pace. Right away, Dave understood how the climb had to be conducted.

"The west flank is ideal for me," I explained. "It's fairly steep rock so I can use my hands most of the time, there's no hot march from the valley to reach the mountain, and I can acclimatise at the Jungfraujoch first."

"I definitely want to go," he told me. "Some of the other lads are interested too. Bloody fools!"

It was too early to count chickens. People could change their minds.

In March 1972, Dave rang me from South Wales.

"You've just been made an honorary life member of the club, Norm, you lucky swine. That's cost you a few pints."

"I'm very pleased."

"We're getting a mini-bus for the summer. Thirteen people, counting you and Judy, going to the Bernese Oberland."

"It's on then?"

"Yes. We haven't decided yet who will be on the rope with you and me, but it may be Len Dacey. He's a good man on the mountains. We'll have to meet up and talk about equipment sometime."

"Yes, we'll need good bivi gear. It's great to hear you can go."

Weeks went by and I sent Dave a letter which sketched the plan for the Eiger. His reply arrived a few weeks later:

Dear Norm and Jude,
Many appologies for not having written

132

before. I'm the worst letter writer imaginable. Helen's got a gun at my head at the moment. How's life with you both? Things are hectic in South Wales, but at least the trip is organised (Helen's job). We like all your plans for the Eiger—Len Dacey will probably be on the rope with us, whilst there will be at least one other rope on the mountain at the same time.

When we get to the Alps I expect a lot of people to be disappearing off to their own routes and huts. I can't wait to get over there again this year. ALPS—here we come.

We will sort out the gear we need as soon as I see you, which I hope is going to be pretty soon now. Helen has to do a computer course in London for a week beginning June 11th. Would it be convenient if we saw you at either end of that week?

I've been made redundant!!! The great unemployment again but have also just been accepted to do a year's Diploma in Education in Cardiff starting next September so I'm not worried. Good old Helen's going to be bread-winner again. I've just vowed I'll never work in industry again.

See you soon. Take care of yourselves.

Dave.

We met in London to make final plans. Dave was helping out temporarily in a mountaineering equipment shop and could get forty per cent off everything we needed—as a result we ordered all we needed and several other things besides.

For a few weeks details of equipment and travelling arrangements sped by post and telephone between Cardiff and London. At the limb centre Brian Campbell checked my legs to ensure that they were mechanically sound. Time dragged. There was no way to make summer come early, and just wanting that to happen seemed to make it take longer. Then it was time to go.

Judy and I were picked up from home one Friday evening near the end of July. We collected three more people from Victoria Station and the party, thirteen in all, was complete.

We reached Grindelwald after one night's camping in France. Six tents were quickly erected on a camp-site overlooked by the Eiger. The camp served as a base from which groups of climbers could go off to huts for a day or two at a time. It was pleasant there, at the top of a grassy meadow, near two big chalets and a wooden barn, and close to a stream which spilled steeply between trees. Huge mountains, just a few miles away, rose ten thousand feet above us.

Everyone tucked in to a meal before an evening spent nosing around the shops and bars of touristy, spick and span, sprawling, expensive Grindelwald.

The next morning I rang Ueli Sommer, the hotel manager at Jungfraujoch, and reserved dormitory places for thirteen for that evening. Although later we would be splitting into smaller groups, none of the party wanted to miss the opportunity of visiting the 11,333 feet (3,454 metres) high Jungfraujoch.

The mountain railway journey was familiar. I wondered how I would be feeling when I made the descent by train to the valley. Would I have proved I could cope with long routes if I bivouacked? On Mont Blanc I had not bivouacked but had stayed in huts. On the Eiger's west flank I would have to bivouac because there are no huts.

Most of the club members chose to climb the Mönch the next day but Judy and I took it easy, preferring not to do much exercise on our first day at high altitude. We strolled out to the base of the Mönch in the early morning and Judy began her training in the use of ice-axe and crampons. She never became enthusiastic about climbing, however, and preferred mountain walking. Apart from one bruised bottom and a broken camera, the club members rerturned unscathed from the Mönch.

The Jungfrau attracted them the next day but once more Judy and I opted out. I had no intention of working hard until I had had two or three nights high up, and Judy did not want to go. After their climb everyone else went down to the valley while Judy and I caught a train to the Eiger Glacier Station Hotel. Dave rang from the valley two days later.

"The weather's bad and Helen's got a face like a football. She was in the sun too long a few days ago," he said.

Judy and I settled down to wait. The daily telephone call from the valley and dinner at six thirty p.m. became the foci of our lives. Mist hung over the mountains and cleared only infrequently to give a view of the west flank, at whose foot the hotel stood. We gazed at the misty mountains and strolled around the alpine pastures below the hotel.

Friday, Saturday, Sunday and Monday crept by. I met Frau Sommer who, with her husband, ran the hotels at Jungfraujoch and Eiger Glacier station.

"If the weather is bad for a long time, can I wash glasses at Jungfraujoch again?" I asked her.

"Of course. We would be pleased to have you back. You can stay in one of the staff rooms like you did last year."

I hoped I would not have to wait long for good weather but it was good to know that there would be work to occupy me if the weather remained unsuitable. There was no harm in planning ahead.

A 'phone call came at midday on August 2nd.

"We're coming up," Dave said. "We should be there at four o'clock."

They arrived on time and Judy caught the train to the valley. We expected the climb to last two days and Judy preferred to wait at the camp site with Dave's wife, Helen, and Len's wife, Robbie. There was no doubt that Judy was apprehensive. In the office where she worked was the widow of a man who was killed on the Eiger.

Dave was bearded, bespectacled and jovial, and had the Welshman's tendency to talk in a high-pitched voice when excited. At the time he weighed a bit more than twelve stone, which looked heavy for a man of five feet eight inches. This was his sixth visit to the Alps and he had wide climbing experience in Britain. He was twenty-eight years old and had just abandoned the career into which his degree in ceramic technology had led him. He was a life-and-soul-of-the-party sort of person, occasionally too much so first thing in the morning. Having once made up his mind on any topic he stuck firmly to his point of view. He was a kind man and more easily hurt than most people realised. The year before he had had a spectacular fall of nearly a hundred and fifty feet in the Alps, but this had not dimmed his enthusiasm. He had fallen over a cliff, pulled the second man off, and Dave's wife was about to disappear over the edge on the end of the rope. With two men already falling fast she could not possibly have held them without a belay, and she had no belay. Then someone on another rope caught her around the waist and held everyone! The friction of the rope over the edge of the cliff must have contributed a great deal towards making such a dramatic saving of life possible. No one had more than minor injuries.

Len Dacey was about thirty years old, quite slim and around five and a half feet tall. He, like Dave, was bearded. His eyes were the features you noticed most about him: brown, and at times fiery, they seemed to explain immediately what the man was all about, showing him at a glance to be sensitive, moody, sincere, intelligent and restless. People found it easy to forgive his bad moods. On the mountains he could move with great speed when he wished, and he had climbed in the Alps for five seasons. He worked as a design engineer.

Excitement gripped us all and we were really living. Over a huge dinner and a few beers we speculated on our chances and were optimistic.

It was nearly ten o'clock when we went to bed, with the intention of sleeping five or six hours. There was no need to start very early because we planned to climb for only six or seven hours before halting to bivouac. A light snow shower had begun but if it stopped soon we could still climb.

I woke up at half past three that morning. It was still snowing and two or three inches of snow lay on the ground. We couldn't go.

There would be too many avalanches and too much powdery snow.

It was not until nine in the morning that we got up and strolled out to look at the west flank. Light snow still fluttered down. What could be seen of the route was whitened all the way. We stood around sighing and swearing for a while, then went back to the hotel.

During the day Kurt, a mountain guide who lived near the hotel, expressed interest in our climb. Birgit, one of the staff, acted as interpreter and told us that if I had no one to climb with Kurt would be prepared to go when the conditions were right. Looking ahead again, that was good news: Len and Dave could wait only a few days before going home.

For three days the sun worked on the west flank to reduce the avalanche-prone snow. Time was short. The mini-bus would leave for England in five days. The west flank was not in good condition because there was far too much ice around. A year before Ueli Sommer had gone on two rescues in the same day on the west flank. Ice had put eight people in danger on that day and one of them had fallen and died. We had no intention of going in conditions which were as bad as on that occasion, but we decided to climb as soon as the weather forecast was favourable. Even if there was quite a lot of ice about it was possible that we could proceed slowly to the summit.

The television weather forecast was good and the sunset turned the mountains pink. With the kit packed, we went to bed.

Stars showed that the weather was clear at four a.m. Herby, chef de service at the hotel, and Birgit had prepared a tray of flasks of coffee, bread, butter and jam the night before. Dave ate sparingly while Len and I made do with sugary coffee. It all seemed a bit unreal to me.

Five o'clock was not many minutes away when we left. Daylight had come by then. It was warm enough with a shirt and a thin sweater. Under a rock beside the well-beaten track across the glacial moraine we hid a few possessions which would not be needed on the mountain.

The rock rose in steps which varied between a few inches and six or eight feet. We would rise up a rock step to a platform, up another step to a platform and so on. Some of the broad platforms sloped and were littered with small stones. We moved unroped, with

Dave leading and Len last. Often I had to scramble, using my hands for balance, where Len and Dave walked. Apart from discussions about which way over the rock looked best, conversation ceased.

The sky graduated from bright blue in the east to dark blue in the west. It took an hour and a half to reach the bottom of the first snowfield that we had to climb. A year before I had estimated it sloped at thirty degrees but looking at it again I reckoned the angle was a little less. The snow stretched farther down the mountain than it had twelve months earlier.

In some circumstances I would have been in the middle but we roped up with me last. It seemed best that Dave, who would lead, should be protected by Len.

Len had a cigarette while we put on crampons. He was a heavy smoker.

The firm snow was just right for Dave to kick steps to stand in, and we followed in his footprints. The snowfield presented no problems and in forty minutes we were on rock again.

Conversation increased, although Len rarely said much. We talked about the route, about the scenery, about the weather, and we were happy.

To our right was a wide gully, or couloir. Frozen streams snaked down the mountain; between them there was no ice. Occasionally we would spot a cairn which marked the way but we would be unable to reach it easily: thick ice coated the rock on the way. The normal route weaved up, traversing frequently to the left and right to avoid the hardest or most dangerous, broken rock. Time and time again we had to abandon what would have been an easy way if there had been less ice.

We must have used the same sentences over and over again.

"That's a cairn over there."

"If we can cross this ice the going looks good on the other side."

"This must be easy without the ice."

"I don't like this bit. Can you find a good belay?"

"It's a pity that slab is so slippery."

"That was a dodgy move."

Now and then we could chop at the ice and clear enough to get a foothold, but this wasted time. Even gently sloping rock was treacherous when covered in the hard, transparent film. Crampons would have helped on the ice but not on clear, sloping slabs. To put crampons on and take them off repeatedly takes time and it was a bother to decide to stop frequently. Looking back, I at least should have worn them more, but that is something which only further experience could tell me.

As we would on a rock climb in Britain, we belayed frequently. The usual way of tackling a route like the west flank, with everyone moving at the same time while roped together, did not seem appropriate in such conditions. I was quite scared sometimes. Once I was hanging on to a large handhold when the whole huge block it was part of moved a quarter of an inch. I was on two small footholds and my other handhold was a tiny crack. I did not enjoy the couple of seconds which elapsed while I transfered my hand to another hold. Above all, I had to avoid falling and landing on my legs.

Shortly after ten o'clock we halted to smear on glacier cream. We were in an area of broken rock with a little danger of stonefall but it was too hot to keep our helmets on.

A party of four men, a bit to our left as we looked down, moved quickly up the rock.

Either they knew the route well or they had been lucky in their route-finding. They had the advantage of not being weighed down with heavy rucksacks, but even allowing for that they were making much better progress. They drew level with us, about three hundred feet away, and one of them called in English.

"It's better over here."

When we carried on we moved in their direction. They were two or three hundred feet above us by then.

We began to sing snatches of pop songs we had heard on the juke box at the Eiger Glacier Station Hotel. Success seemed likely, even in those quite bad conditions.

We kept to rock as far as possible, following little ribs, surmounting small, easy cliffs and scrambling up slabs of loose rock which fractured under our boots. Mostly it was not steep or difficult, but in places we felt uncomfortable.

"This is the sort of place where you get the chop if you're clumsy," Dave said.

It was plain to see that in good conditions the climbing was not hard, but the ice made a tremendous difference. However, like the vast majority of climbing parties on the west flank we carried on without incident.

In every direction were ferns of frost, displayed over rock like the most delicate of silver jewellery. Snow lay in cracks and places shielded from the sun, and occasionally we climbed for a few feet in a narrow gully. Wherever possible it was better to avoid the snow because it had become soft. Avalanches thundered down neighbouring mountains but we were not threatened.

The route took us up and to the left, towards the north face. It became a plod, up an easy angled rock and along wide ledges which had collected small stones.

Suddenly we were on the edge of the north face: vertical rock sections and steep icefields. We stared and said, "Bloody hell!" for a long time.

The place where we stood was familiar. It was there that we had turned back on my first attempt on the west flank. Treas had called this Frühstückplatze, but another guide told me later that Frühstückplatze was the name given to an area lower on the mountain. The first time it had taken four and a half hours to get that far; this time we had climbed for six and a half hours. Heavy rucksacks had slowed us, but most of all the ice had been the

146

enemy, forcing us several times to leave the route.

Len sat and had a cigarette. Dave and I ate a little chocolate.

"We must be over half-way now," one of them remarked.

"No. Not yet," I said. "This is where we turned back last year."

When we talked of half-way we were trying to judge the height. Some mountains rise irregularly and the difficulties may be concentrated in one short section, not necessarily near the top. The Eiger west flank rises fairly regularly and the climbing is roughly consistent throughout, so height gained was a guide to our progress.

"How are your stumps, Norm?" Dave asked.

"They feel fine."

"We could keep on for an hour or two, then?"

It was Len who asked.

"Certainly," I told him. "I'm surprised, but the stumps are not very sore. Usually six and a half hours climbing knocks them about."

"It's not been easy going, either," Dave

said. "I don't mind admitting I was gripped a couple of times."

"Gripped" means "scared" to a climber. Some would say "terrified" is nearer the mark.

We climbed for two hours. In hindsight, I can see that a better knowledge of the route would have helped us over this section. The guide-book description contained little detail. The rock we climbed could have been avoided. Belaying as much as possible, we headed slowly upwards until at half past one we reached a broad, snow-covered ledge.

"Good bivi spot," Dave said. "And it's about two-thirds of the way up."

Len thought we were near two-thirds of the way up too.

"I don't think we're much above half way," I remarked. I meant it as a comment but it sounded like a moan.

"We've been climbing for nearly nine hours," Dave said. "If you're going to climb for long tomorrow you'll have to stop now."

"That's true," I agreed. "I didn't intend moving for longer than six or seven hours. What do you think, Len?"

"We'll be lucky to find as good a bivi site if we carry on. I think we should stop. We can dump most of our gear here and climb light tomorow."

"All right," I said. I was tired and glad to stop. I estimated that we were ten and a half thousand feet up.

The ledge was about ten feet wide and twenty feet long. At one end the north face fell away vertically. We were pleased to find such a big step in the ridge because there was room to put up our bivouac tent. With ice-axes we chopped a level space in the snow and erected the shelter. Six feet eight inches long, three feet ten inches wide and two feet eight inches at its highest, it was made for two people but we planned to fit three in. In case the wind increased we hammered pitons into the rock and attached several guy-lines to our blue nylon "dog kennel".

Len started to boil water for tea on a stove which was protected from breeze by a circular windshield of snow.

Kleine Scheidegg stood nearly four thousand feet below and Grindelwald was over seven thousand feet lower than us. It was warm, clear and sunny, and peak after peak showed itself as far as the horizon. If you were told to make something beautiful from grey, brown and black rock and some snow you might think the task impossible, yet nature has succeeded countless times in the mountains.

The party of four people who passed us earlier had been sitting on rocks a few hundred feet higher. They began to descend.

We drank tea and admired the view. Some pretty butterflies (red and brown and yellow, I think) skimmed by. I don't know if they were local residents but if they were, they must have adapted to terrible weather conditions.

The four men descended to our bivouac site. One of them was English and I believe his companions were French. They reckoned they had been within six hundred feet of the summit but we discovered later that the highest point at which we had seen them was about two thousand feet below the top. They explained that they had just been lucky in finding a good route. They were not experienced and did not know the route well. After wishing us luck they resumed their descent.

The sun warmed us and we idled the afternoon away. I got some more tea going at four o'clock and a couple of hours later we cooked beef stew and drank mugs of hot beef extract.

Dave puffed on his pipe and Len smoked

cigarettes. The sound of huskies whining reached us from the Eiger Glacier station and the doleful notes of an alpenhorn drifted up from Kleine Scheidegg. Brightly painted small planes buzzed between the peaks. The gradual darkening of the deep, green valleys towards sunset heightened the glorious pink glow of the snowy mountains. Close by, a clear stream splashed and sprayed its course down. It was an enchanted evening.

"We should make good speed tomorrow," Dave forecasted.

"We can leave the tent up and stop here again when we get back from the top," Len said.

It grew cold. We put on down jackets and prepared to go to bed. The rucksacks were tied to a piton outside the tent.

I was first into the tent so I could take my legs off and wash the stumps. I examined them for broken skin.

"Good grief!" I exclaimed.

"What's up?" Dave asked from outside.

"My stumps."

"What's wrong with them?"

"Nothing. Nothing at all. They're perfect. It's nearly a miracle."

No split skin, no chafing, no bruising, no

bleeding, no swelling. I had never climbed for nearly nine hours without some trouble.

"It must be these nylon stump socks," I explained.

Len crawled into the tent to spread out his sleeping bag. He took off his boots, then kicked over my small plastic bowl of water.

"Bloody 'ell! It's all over my socks. They're soaked," he said.

The problem was easily solved: I put on his wet socks because it did not matter to me, and he took mine.

Len and I settled down in our sleeping bags and called to Dave, "Come in, Twiggy."

It was a tight squeeze but we all managed to find a fairly comfortable position to lie in. By eight o'clock the light was fading quickly. Fine weather tempted us to believe that we would reach the summit the next day. The night was not cold.

Cough, cough, cough, cough. The morning sounds of Len and Dave getting up were as unpleasant as an alarm clock. Five o'clock. Clear sky.

Dave sat on a rock outside the tent and made some tea.

"Anything wrong with your legs, Norm?" he asked.

"No."

"Pity. We could have used that as an excuse to go down."

He was not serious. There was nothing but ourselves to stop us going down.

I mentioned that if I could not make it they could go to the top while I waited, but they refused to consider the idea.

"We're doing this as a team," Dave said.

At six o'clock we moved off. Frozen streams hung down the mountain and restricted our choice of route once more. We were soon on rock which we thought would be graded as Difficult. It was harder than we should have encountered on that part of the route. Some days later I discovered that the rock was much easier to climb on our right, on the far side of a broad, frozen stream.

On tiny holds we picked our way up the rock. The angle was probably less than fifty degrees but we were uncomfortable again. Sometimes, strung out at the full 150 feet of the rope, we couldn't find one good belay anchor between us. Thin splinters of rock scraped and crackled underfoot.

"I'm not coming down this bit," Len remarked definitely.

Dave led with great care. He was silent

when he concentrated and chatted when he was relaxed.

"This is like climbing in the Avon Gorge," he said. "I like it! I like it!"

In an hour we had risen only three or four hundred feet. Icicle beards hung from the rock, to tinkle down if we brushed past. Two Englishmen passed us, going well. Two more climbers reached our tent at about half past eight and turned back, probably because they found they were slowed by the ice.

There was a visual disappointment: the Silberhorn, a magnificent snow cone near the Jungfrau, looked flatter and less impressive as we gained height.

Weaving through snow-cloaked boulders, we arrived at the bottom of a snowfield. In three and a half hours we had not risen more than six or seven hundred feet. We sat to put on gloves and crampons, and two German-speaking climbers caught up with us. They waited for us to climb.

Len took the lead because he had more snow and ice experience. There was a step of nearly vertical ice, ten or twelve feet high, in front. I suggested we should look around for a better way on to the snowfield but we could not see one.

Len chipped out a couple of footholds with his ice hammer, a tool with a long pick for cutting into ice. His crampons bit in the holds he had made. He moved up a short way and embedded his ice hammer in the ice as a handhold, then found an icy hold for his left hand and used the front points of his right crampon. The ice hammer dug in higher up and his left crampon came up and bit home. With one or two more movements he was standing on the snowfield.

Dave followed and I got up with less effort than I anticipated.

The German-speaking pair watched us and wandered off below the snowfield, presumably hoping to find an easier way on to it.

"Must be quite close to the top now," Dave said.

"Yes. Not far now," Len agreed.

I could not share their optimism but did not voice my opinion. The Eiger is a deceptive mountain, like many: viewed from Kleine Scheidegg, prominent features which are two thousand feet below the summit appear to be within five hundred feet of the top.

Estimating the angle of a snowfield is not easy but I think this one was about forty degrees. I suppose it was four hundred feet from top to bottom. The snow was a bit on the soft side and rather likely to avalanche, I felt. We plodded steadily up. I had two ice-axes and soon got into a rhythm—left axe forward, then the right leg, right axe forward, then the left leg. Part way up the snowfield we could probably have moved to the rock on our right, but we were not sure. We kept to the snow. For safety I would have preferred the rock.

It was essential to keep an eye on the weather, to retreat immediately if it turned bad, or we would be in trouble.

Above the snowfield was a cliff. To avoid it we went to the right. I knew Dave and Len thought we were quite close to the summit. It looked as if we would soon see how close when we skirted around the cliff and gained a little height.

We rounded a corner and our hearts must have sunk at the same time. We were not even as high as the ridge which ran between the Mönch and the Eiger. At the lowest point that ridge was more than a thousand feet below the Eiger. At a rough guess I put us one thousand five hundred feet below the summit of the Eiger.

"Oh, hell!" Dave said.

For a minute or two we stood and looked around before tramping up a forty-five degree slope of snow. The slope had been exposed to the sun for several hours and had lost its firmness. Each minute seemed long as we struggled on.

Midday was near. Dave stopped.

"It's time we talked about what we're going to do," he said. "I'm not saying we should turn back but we ought to take stock now."

The snow stretched up for several hundred feet and at the top of the snow was steep rock. I couldn't pick out the summit. A thousand feet to go? More, I thought.

"What do you think, Len?" Dave asked.

"We can't stop now."

"How about you, Norm?" Dave enquired, turning to me. "The snows bad enough as it is. It's going to be worse by the time we come down."

I slipped my rucksack off and sat on it.

"I think we should let Norman make the decision," Dave added.

"O.K." Len agreed. "He knows how he's feeling."

"Hold on then," I said. "Give me a couple of minutes. I want to be sure that if we do

157

turn back I won't find myself regretting the decision tomorrow."

Did we have to abandon all hope of success? The snow was soft and would have become softer; there would be an increasing danger of avalanche, particularly on the descent. Even the snow we stood on could have slipped away. The final snow to the summit would be hazardous, too. Descent on soft snow was my weak point. Considering the average rate at which we had climbed over two days, to reach the summit we had to allow four more hours of ascent. To be on the safe side I would have to assume that my rate of descent to the tent might be as slow as my rate of ascent. Adding it all up, I had to reckon on ten hours of ascent and ten hours of descent—twenty hours of climbing in one day. It was clearly unwise to go on. Even to turn back immediately, I told myself, could mean a twelve-hour day. Wishing the facts to be different did not alter them.

"We should go down," I said. I had had my doubts about reaching the summit so I was not suddenly disappointed. For Dave and Len it was worse.

The snow was noticeably worse as we descended but the ice was quickly melting to make the rocks easy to climb. If we had been able to start two days later the rock would have been almost free of ice.

A five pound rock, toppled by our rope, bounced and spun down the mountain. We shouted to warn anyone beneath.

Taking our time, we were back at the tent in four hours.

"Let's have a brew," Len said, starting to make tea.

I sat on a rock and nodded off to sleep for a few minutes. Len woke me when the tea was ready. I think we had all pictured what it would be like when we returned from a successful ascent. As we sipped our tea, the reality made a sad contrast.

"I'm pissed off," Dave announced. "But we made the right decision."

"I'm sure we did," I agreed. "Anyway, we haven't totally wasted our time. We've had a couple of interesting days, and I reckon we were a thousand feet or perhaps more from the top. The climbing isn't usually much harder farther up, so that shows we could have done it in good conditions. It's nice to be in the mountains anyway."

"You going to try again?" Len asked me.

"I think so. It's a pity you two can't stay for a few more days."

"I'm tempted," Len said. "I can't stay, though. Will you look for a guide?"

"Yes. One or two. Kurt wants to go."

I had hoped to climb the Eiger with friends rather than guides, and whether I went with friends or guides the mechanical effort required of me would be the same. However, there was one advantage of taking a guide: we would not be slowed by route-finding problems.

We sat quietly and stared at the valley. Our wives had come up to the Eiger Glacier station and were watching through a telescope as we arrived back at the bivouac site. From their viewpoint it looked as if we had bivouacked two-thirds of the way up the route so they believed all had gone according to plan. Judy started writing joyful postcards to friends and relations but fortunately she decided not to post them until she had confirmed the good news.

"There's beer down there," Len said at last. "When I'm in the valley all I want to do is get up here, and when I'm up here I want to get down there. It's crazy."

"We haven't seen the women for five days," Dave remarked.

We thought of the things we were missing. Ours was a dismal group. The snow platform under the tent had melted away, leaving us on a lumpy stone mattress.

The tent and other equipment was packed up by half past seven the next day.

"How are your stumps?" Dave asked.

"A bit sore, but not too bad."

Much to our annoyance we found that the ice had melted away to leave a route which we could have climbed in half the time. Higher up it was probably still quite icy but not as bad as when we were there. Time and time again we recognised places that were so slippery on the ascent that we could climb them only with great difficulty. Now we could saunter down.

We were descending an easy section of rock where we could scramble, facing outwards. Occasionally we needed to put our hands to the rock to balance. I was leading the way with Len at the rear. Suddenly we heard a cry, almost a scream.

"Aagh!"

Out of the corner of my eye I saw Dave shoot forward and down. We had the rope tight and I threw myself back on the rock, waiting for the strain. He was quite heavy, and we had no belays.

Dave stayed where he was.

"It's all right," he said cheerily. "I wasn't falling. I sat on the pick of my ice hammer."

Going down the lowest snowfield was enjoyable because I slid while Len and Dave held the rope to make sure I didn't get out of control. We had to stop once when my left leg started to come off. I can't understand how it happened because I was sliding feet first, but the stump was nearly out of the socket by the time I halted.

Below the snowfield we sat around for a while and the two German-speaking climbers we saw the day before caught up with us. They had reached the summit and been forced to bivouac high up. They had run out of fuel for their stove and spent a very uncomfortable night during which one of them sat for hours with frozen socks. We gave them a cylinder of gas and they went to make a hot drink in their tent, which they had left near the bottom of the snowfield. The broken wooden shaft on one of their ice-axes persuaded me to buy an axe with a metal shaft when I got home.

After unroping, we ambled down. It took about four hours to make the descent from the bivi site. Helen, Robbie and Judy met us near the Eiger Glacier station. They were surprised and sorry to hear our news.

Back at the camp-site that evening I discovered that my right foot was loose. The movement was not great but it was too much for me to attempt the Eiger again without having it corrected. Three choices faced me: I could try to find someone in Switzerland who could tackle the job, I could go back to England for my other right leg and then return to Switzerland, or I could give up. If I chose the last course I had an easy excuse, that my artificial legs would not stand up to the work. However, I didn't believe that. The looseness of the foot was so slight that I could possibly have climbed for days without trouble, but I didn't want to risk having a foot falling off when I was half-way up the mountain.

A local doctor gave me the address of a firm which repaired artificial limbs but the information proved to be out of date. After much hunting I found, listed in the telephone directory as orthopaedic appliance manufacturers, the address of Botta and Sons at Biel. When I rang them they agreed to take a look at the limb.

Bad weather had prevented most of the group from climbing more than one or two peaks in the whole holiday and they were pleased to pack up and go home. We bade goodbye to a thousand earwigs which had camped with us, and left Grindelwald.

The homeward route passed close to Biel so we made a small detour and found Botta's premises. A man there examined the limb and put it right in a few minutes, much to my relief.

At Biel station we made our farewells before I caught a train back to Grindelwald.

"Pity you have to go home," I said to Len and Dave.

They were both tempted to stay but had to go back to work.

Judy looked as if I were about to play football in a minefield. She was not usually so anxious when I climbed.

"You could be home in five or six days," she said. "All you need is good weather and a couple of guides."

6

GOOD weather and a couple of guides. It started to rain just after I reached Grindelwald. I rang Birgit at the Eiger Glacier Station Hotel to ask if she knew where Kurt, the guide, was.

"He has to go into the army for three weeks," she said.

"That's a pity."

"You should go to the guides' office in Grindelwald, and see if they can find someone."

At the guides' office I explained to the woman in charge about hiring two guides who would bivouac for at least one night. On a postcard, I showed her where Len, Dave and I turned back. The woman asked me to telephone her in two days.

From the dormitory where I stayed, over the station buffet at Kleine Scheidegg, I could see the Eiger. A hundred times I climbed the west flank with my eyes. Experience had taught me to be patient about the things I could not change, but that did not mean I enjoyed waiting. I wanted this ambition behind me so I could climb without such urgency, for sheer pleasure.

The time came to ring the guides' office and the woman asked me to contact a guide, Hans Kaufmann, by telephone.

It took several calls that afternoon before I caught Herr Kaufmann at home in Grindelwald. In slow and clear English he began to question me.

"You are the man who wants to climb the west flank?" he asked.

"Yes."

"Is it right that you have no legs?"

"Yes. Below the knees."

"How did you get on before on the west flank?"

"Very slowly. There was too much ice. I was with two friends who had to go back to England. We started a day or two too early."

"What is hardest for you?"

"Going on soft snow."

He asked how long the various stages had taken me on Mont Blanc and I told him.

"How long can you climb?"

"Last time I climbed for nine hours on one day and ten hours the next day. I could go on for longer but I think that would be unwise in normal circumstances."

"We could take bivouac equipment with us and if you are going well on the first day we can leave that equipment part way up the mountain and go on to the summit."

"Maybe. But we'll have to bivouac once."

I did not want him to think I could manage without bivouacking. He was silent for a few seconds. Had I put him off by insisting that we would bivouac?

"I will find another guide for when the weather is very good," he said.

"Thank you. I'm pleased."

That was an understatement!

The weather was bad at the time so I decided to go to the hotel at the Jungfraujoch to wash glasses and acclimatise. If it were not for that job I would have been unable to have afforded to wait for long.

Ueli was talking about the west flank one day when he said, "I think maybe it is too much for you."

Judging from how I climbed two years before when I went up the Mönch with him, I would have come to the same conclusion. But now I could move more quickly, and the rock of the west flank would suit me.

"I think you will maybe get up all right but you have to get down and that will not be easy for you," he said.

"I can climb for much longer than I could two years ago," I explained. "There's still a lot of room for improvement but the more I practice the easier it becomes."

Two days later Hans Almer, the guide with whom I had climbed the Jungfrau, used the same words as Ueli.

"I think the Eiger is too much for you."

He and Ueli had no way of knowing how much I had improved in two years, and the nylon stump socks seemed to have removed, or at least greatly reduced, the likelihood of the sort of physical damage I had suffered on Mont Blanc. That was a critical factor.

Four weeks after leaving England I was waiting for good weather while a blizzard raged outside. That meant the west flank would take a few more days to come into condition. The news was not all bad: Herr Kaufmann had found another guide to accompany us.

I met Hans Kaufmann one day at Jungfraujoch. He was thirty-five years old, younger than I had judged from his voice on the telephone. He was broad, ruddy-complexioned and heavy featured. He was a farmer, I was told, who guided during the summer. He seemed like someone who made up his own mind and went his own way.

"We could go in three or four days if the weather is good," he told me. But it did not improve, except for short periods.

September came. Six weeks had elapsed since I left home. Six weeks and still I hadn't got up! Sunday, September 3rd, was not a happy day. In the morning I saw that it had been snowing quite heavily. I had to face it—my chances of making another attempt on the Eiger in 1972 were small. The season was drawing to a close. The Eiger Station Hotel was due to shut down in a few days until the ski season. A fast, able-bodied party could contemplate ascents for a few weeks because they would not have to bivouac; taking my planned bivouac into account, I reckoned that there might be about two weeks left to attempt a route like the west flank. It would take a few days of that fortnight for the recent snow to clear.

One Sunday evening the television weather forecast was good. Within ten minutes Hans Kaufmann rang.

"The forecast is good," I told him.

"I know. I will ring the other guide. We need two or three days of good weather. If it is all right we can go to the Eiger Glacier Station Hotel on Wednesday and climb on Thursday."

Monday was hot and the fresh snow melted quickly from rocks in front of the hotel. Tuesday was hot as well.

The station master at Jungfraujoch was always a helpful man. When I asked him if he had any insulation tape he contacted an electrician who gave me some. I wound the tape and long strands of nylon string around my feet and legs to strengthen them.

Early on Wednesday morning it was snowing lightly but the shower was brief. Once more I rang Hans Kaufmann, who suggested we should wait until noon to see how the weather turned out. If it was fine we could go to the Eiger Station Hotel the same day.

The glass washing machine droned away in the little room where I worked. At a quarter-past twelve the 'phone rang. It was Hans Balmer, the second guide.

"What do you think about the weather, Hans?"

"Well, I think the weather will be good.

We can start at two o'clock tomorrow morning."

The train ride down through the tunnel felt like the beginning of an adventure. The tension of waiting subsided. I found it difficult to believe that the weather could get worse again in a few hours.

After sorting through my equipment at the Eiger Glacier Station Hotel I left what was not needed with Barry, an English chef. Then I slept for a couple of hours.

Two journalists from a Swiss magazine were waiting in the restaurant when I went down for dinner. While we ate they conducted an interview about the proposed climb. Nearly an hour went by and someone said the last train had come up from Kleine Scheidegg. The guides had not arrived. Anxious minutes dragged by. Much to my relief, there was another train and they were on it. I introduced the two journalists, Richard and Franz, and the guides sat down for dinner.

Hans Balmer was twenty-six years old and looked more like a fit, blond German than a Swiss of the Bernese Oberland. He was often silent, unlike his older friend, Hans Kaufmann. They were both strong farmers and had more sense of humour than most of their neighbours.

Richard and Franz had had some mountaineering experience and wanted to accompany our party to take pictures on the west flank. Hans Kaufmann pointed out that with no crampons, ice-axes or rope they should not go far. They were very disappointed about not having their climbing equipment with them.

Birgit asked if I thought I could manage the climb without a bivouac and I told her I was certain I could not. Within twelve hours I would learn the significance of her question.

The guides and I went up to our room to sort out equipment. I kept an eye open for articles of bivouac equipment and they had plenty. They brought torches, stoves, matches, fuel, food and ample warm clothing. We each had a nylon bivi-bag.

I went to bed and fell asleep before the guides turned in.

The light flashed on in the room shortly after one a.m.

"Time to get up!" Birgit called to the three of us.

We all dressed quickly and, taking our rucksacks with us, went downstairs to the restaurant. The usual breakfast was a flask or two of coffee with bread, butter and jam, but we were in for a surprise. Birgit was serving bacon and eggs. Soon the unexpected breakfast party grew to a dozen people, including several of the railway workers, a two-man television team and Richard and Franz. The railway staff had been drinking until then and were in high spirits, in contrast to my mood of quiet nervousness. Within two days I would know the outcome of the attempt. If I failed there would perhaps be an opportunity to try again in a year's time but I was eager to grab the ascent.

Franz, Richard, the guides and I sat at the same table.

"We wish we were coming with you," Richard said. "Not just for the photographs but for the climbing as well. Now we must be content to watch you through the telescope outside. We will wait until you come down."

"How do you feel?" Franz asked me.

"Fine, thanks. A bit nervous."

"I want to take some pictures as you leave and also I will make a short interview for the television," Richard explained.

"The weather looks all right," Hans Kaufmann remarked.

While we ate, people laughed, talked loudly in German and tottered about. No one was tired and this was the noisiest early morning start I could remember.

With the last of the bacon and eggs and tea finished, the guides and I hoisted up our rucksacks and went outside. It was not very cold.

"It is a bit too warm," Hans Kaufmann said. The snow, particularly as we went higher, would not be in the best condition.

Torches were switched on and several people accompanied us over the first two or three hundred yards of track. The T.V. crew set up some powerful lights and Richard took still photographs before recording a short interview.

"We will make another interview when you come down," he said. It crossed my mind that I would not look forward to the interview if I failed once more to reach the summit. What a miserable occasion such an interview would be!

After the special breakfast and the recording, we did not set off until nearly three o'clock. Hans Kaufmann led the way and Hans Balmer followed me. Like a pair of cinema usherettes they shone their torches where I put my boots. They did that job well.

"Do you want the rope?" Hans Kaufmann asked me when we reached steps of rock.

"I'm happy to go unroped for a while. The rock is dry and easy to climb."

My two companions conversed in German. "I hope you don't mind us talking in German," Hans Kaufmann said. "We are deciding which way to go. It is not easy to find in the dark."

"No, that's fine. I don't chat much when I'm climbing anyway."

I suspected that as well as discussing the route they were weighing up my chances of reaching the summit. If they were not it was surprising, because they had not seen me climb before.

Breathing was no problem because I had acclimatised. Outlines of mountains could just be discerned against the sky, but without torches we could not have seen the grey rock where we climbed. Snow and ice avalanches and rockfalls that we heard were all a long way off. A stream gushed down to our right. The night was full of the noises of rock, snow, ice and water heading relentlessly downhill.

The rock steps were familiar: up five feet,

almost level for ten feet, up three feet, straight ahead for seven feet, up eight feet, level for twenty feet, and so on. Even though near vertical in places, each step had sufficient holds to give easy climbing. We neared the top of the steps when Hans Balmer stopped to pass me one end of a five-yard piece of rope.

"It is better if you put a rope on now," he said. "In the dark it is not easy."

He went ahead, trailing a few feet of rope behind him, and watched every move I made on the next short, steep sections.

"He can give you a pull on the rope if you ask him," Hans Kaufmann told me.

I said nothing. I did not mind a tight rope in any place where I thought I might fall but I did not like to be helped up.

Ten minutes past four. We were strapping on crampons at the bottom of the snowfield. We roped up with me in the middle. The snow was reasonably firm and Hans Kaufmann kicked steps with ease. We curved a little to the right at first, then climbed straight up the snow.

I tried to keep my thoughts on the climbing of the moment, rather than thinking ahead to the summit. Somehow the time would pass and in four or five hours I would have a good idea of the chances of success: by then we could be aiming to reach the summit the same day. Or would we have decided to turn back because I moved too slowly? I concentrated on going at a reasonably fast pace in the hope that we would be in a good position in a few hours. Contrary to my expectations I did not bring up the egg and bacon. Because of the extreme effort of climbing, a feeling of nausea was often with me.

The light was not strong enough for us to start over the snow without torches but the sky began to grow brighter as we approached the top of the snowfield. The torches were switched off. We crunched ahead, crossing an icy, ten feet wide channel left by an avalanche slipping down, probably days earlier. The avalanche chute presented no danger and we found an easy place to step over the gap between the top of the snowfield and the rock. The two hours we had taken was twenty minutes less than on the previous attempt.

In a minute or two our crampons were off and we were scrambling upwards to the left of a wide and deep gully. Daylight strengthened rapidly. We walked with little effort along ledges which had given trouble to

Dave, Len and me. Now we stepped over little streams which trickled quietly and spread themselves to a width of a foot or two. A month before they had been yards wide and frozen in the morning. While traversing a ledge I could keep one hand on the rock for balance, and that suited me.

The weather was fine. Most of the rock was dry. There were only rare patches of ice to be seen. I began to feel optimistic. The guides were in good humour.

In an hour and a quarter we climbed from the top of the snowfield to the place Treas Schluneggar had called Frühstückplatze. The same section had taken over four hours with Len and Dave. What had been quite hard climbing had turned out an easy scramble when there was no ice.

"Frühstückplatze," I said.

"This is not Frühstückplatze," Hans Kaufmann said. He pointed the way we had come. "Frühstückplatze is down there. Can you keep going like you have done?"

"I think so, or nearly as fast."

"That is good."

With a remarkable view across the north face, this was a natural place to rest. We then took no more than half an hour to reach the spot where I bivouacked with Len and Dave. In three and three-quarter hours from the Eiger Glacier Station we covered the section of the route which had taken eight hours and forty minutes the time before. The difference was due mostly to ice.

"This is about half-way," Hans Kaufmann said soon after we passed the former bivi site. That meant we were about ten and a half thousand feet high.

A little later he said, "We will leave your rucksack. We can reach the top today and come down here to bivouac. If you do not want to get down this far Hans and I will come and carry your rucksack up to you."

"Sounds all right. I may not be able to descend as far as this today if we do get to the summit. All the way up and half-way down in one day is pushing it for me."

I lodged the rucksack under a big boulder. Several other boulders in the vicinity were large enough to provide weather protection if we chose to bivouac under them.

"How are you feeling?" Hans Kaufmann asked.

"I feel in great form."

"And your legs?"

"The stumps seem to be undamaged."

Hans Balmer grinned and made a remark in German. The only word I understood was "champagne".

Having left the rucksack behind I could keep up a good pace. We scrambled between boulders. Where Len, Dave and I chose to climb a snowfield it had become possible to pick an easy route over rock beside the snow.

When it became necessary to traverse the top of the snowfield from left to right below a huge cliff, Hans Kaufmann found a good rock belay and paid out the rope while Hans Balmer kicked steps. This time I was sure my estimate of the angle of the slope, just under fifty degrees, was close. We could see the first twenty-five feet of the humped slope until it disappeared around a corner. Hans Kaufmann kept an eye on his partner while he talked to me.

"Many people say we are crazy to climb with you, but they say we are crazy anyway."

"What did the other guides say?"

"Mostly they say you cannot climb the Eiger. They say it is not possible."

"Why did you and Hans think it was possible?"

"Well, I talked to you about what you have done before so I thought you could do it. We have even bet a bottle of champagne that you will go up and down in one day."

"With Birgit?"

"Yes."

She's won, I thought, and it disturbed me a little to think that after all my explanations the two guides still believed I could manage the Eiger without bivouacking once. It was a long way to the summit, let alone back to the hotel.

"I think I will have to biovouac on the way down," I stressed.

"We will see."

"How long do you think it will take to the summit from here?"

"More than two hours. Perhaps much more."

It was not many minutes past eight o'clock. Hans Balmer climbed until he was out of sight behind the hump of the snowfield. The rope dragged behind him for a few seconds, then he called out for me to follow. I faced the slope, grasped an ice-axe in my right hand and punched handholds in the firm snow with the left hand. After a few sideways steps I found it easier to use two ice-axes. Hans Kaufmann had his good rock belay and Hans

181

Balmer had an ice-axe belay. It was a safe way to cross the snow.

Hans Kaufmann followed after I crossed and we were soon on rock again. Much of the snow that had been around a month before had melted away.

We passed the place at which Len, Dave and I turned back. My final estimate of the height there was thirteen hundred feet below the summit; with no prominent landmarks to use as reference points, this was a very rough estimate.

The sun beat down but a gentle breeze kept us cool. Once or twice an hour we stopped for a minute while one of the guides took photographs.

"It is not possible," Hans Kaufmann said in German. Then he said in English, "He cannot climb the Eiger."

"It is not possible," I echoed in German. Those were the only words of German I learned during the climb.

"Champagne!" Hans Balmer called out.

"Champagne!" the other Hans shouted.

It crossed my mind that it was a bit early for such confidence, but it must have been a relief for them to see we were progressing as fast as I said we might. I reminded myself that there was quite a long way to go and slackened the pace a little.

At the Eiger Glacier station some of the railway and hotel staff, and Franz and Richard, were taking turns to watch through a big telescope. Clear weather allowed them a perfect view. Almost the whole route could be seen.

White scratch marks showed us where people had climbed the rock with crampons when it was icy. The angle varied a few degrees above and below forty. It was easy as there was hardly any ice. Every so often we came across pitons hammered into cracks. We did not need them but on a descent in icy conditions they would have been used as abseil anchors.

The rock rose monotonously for a hundred feet, two hundred, three hundred, five hundred.

"It is not possible," we all said many times.

The route wended again towards the north face. We climbed on the very edge of a mile of rock which approached the vertical. On our left the drop was exciting and awesome at the same time.

The breeze became strong so we put on jackets, hats and gloves.

Hans Balmer went ahead in a small, steep gully. As he ascended stones clattered around him every second or two, but fortunately none of them was large. He climbed thirty feet up the right bank of the gully as we looked at it and threw a rope down.

"We can go quickly if we hold that rope," Hans Kaufmann said. "Climb with your feet and pull on the rope."

We were all tied together with the normal rope which holds someone who falls, but in this case Hans Kaufmann and I made use of the extra rope to pull ourselves up. On many long routes the use of fixed ropes in this way has become common and saves a great deal of time. Little stones bounced past as we hauled on the rope. We left the rope hanging down the gully so we could descend quickly.

The summit was in sight, separated from us by a few hundred feet of rock ridge and then a ridge of snow. An hour to go, I thought.

Surely we could not fail? The weather was all right, and I was not tired. What could stop us? Dangerously soft conditions on the final snowfield, stonefall, or injury from a fall. The risks from stonefall or a fall were remote. So, it depended on the snowfield. "It's a bit too warm," Hans Kaufmann had said on leaving the hotel. Yes, it depended on the snowfield.

"It's not possible!" Hans Kaufmann sang.

"Champagne!" his friend yelled. "Champagne!"

We followed the rock ridge. No ice. Easy climbing. Plenty of holds. Ledges and steps of a few feet and rock sloping gently. Brittle stones crunched under our boots.

Soon all the rock was behind, apart from a small mound visible at the summit. We put on crampons. Ahead, a snow ridge at forty degrees or less. It looked about a hundred yards long. We started to climb. Hans Balmer took the lead. I kept my eyes down on the snow, watching where I was going. Right axe, left leg, left axe, right leg, right axe. The snow was far from firm.

"It will be dangerous here in an hour or two," Hans Kaufmann said. "The snow is getting soft. If you fell you would be finished."

Right leg, right axe, left leg, left axe. Minutes went by. I took a peep at the summit. It seemed as far away as it had five minutes before. A trail of bootprints behind proved we had risen a long way.

Left leg, left axe, right, right, left, left, right, right. I drew deep breaths easily. We moved fast, eagerly. I kept my head down. The angle of the slope was constant, then it lessened quite suddenly. I noticed there were some rocks at the same height as us on the right, ten feet away, and then I saw that we could not go any farther. We were on the summit. In front, the south-east face plunged. From the right and left sharp ridges of rock and snow met at the summit, 13,026 feet (3,970 metres) high. Was I dreaming or was I really there? For a moment it was difficult to appreciate the reality.

The guides shook hands with me.

"Thank you both," I said. "I'm delighted to be here."

They deserved more thanks than I put into words.

It was half past eleven. A number of guides had told me they reckoned to take six or six and a half hours with a client, so I was not dissatisfied at reaching the summit in eight and a half hours.

There was great excitement amongst the onlookers at the Eiger Glacier station. I was glad they could witness the event because some of them had given me a great deal of encouragement. It was a pity that Len and Dave were not on the top too.

The guides took photographs and I picked up a few small stones for Judy. The rock was black and brittle.

The deteriorating snow dictated that we should descend quickly so we rested only briefly. To the south and east, fluffy white clouds added soft lines to a mountain wilderness, and I would have liked more time to sit and stare.

"How do you feel?" Hans Kaufmann enquired.

"Not bad. A bit tired but in three or four hours we can stop where we will bivouac."

"I think you will get back to the hotel today."

"We'll see. It will be more sensible for me to bivouac, I expect."

My stumps were sore but felt as if they were not bleeding.

"We must leave here now," Hans Kaufmann said.

I hoped that after an easy descent of four hours we could bivouac at least half-way down the route. I felt sure that until then I could maintain reasonable concentration.

However, things did not work out as I thought they would.

The sun had been relentlessly at work: the snow towards the bottom of the ridge was noticeably softer less than an hour after we had passed over it on the ascent. It was dangerous and I was not at ease until we left the snowfield behind.

There was no need to hurry. Hans Kaufmann led the way down the rock. Heat made the descent tedious but I was too contented to take much notice of physical discomfort.

"It is not possible," we joked. "Champagne!"

We drew level with two ascending climbers. From their speech I took them to be English. They asked where the summit was and Hans Kaufmann pointed it out. As they plodded on I wondered how they would manage on that final snow ridge, which they would reach nearly two hours later than us.

The rope we had left behind hung down the gully and provided an easy means of descent. Quite soon we passed the place where Dave, Len and I turned back. I was sure we had made the right decision in not carrying on to the summit.

After picking a way down the hot, barren

rock for two hours we were faced with the steep snowfield we had traversed on the way up. Hans Kaufmann went across the unreliable snow and reached the rock belay anchor he had used before. I edged across the soft white mass and was pleased that our route was mostly on rock. At the far side some snow had melted, leaving a gap four or five feet wide. Hans Kaufmann skipped over and turned to me.

"Can you jump?"

"Not far. No feet, no ankles, no calf muscles."

"Can you jump this?"

The snow was a foot lower on the far side of the gap. That was an advantage but I had to jump much more than four feet across because I could not take off from or land on the edges of the slushy snow.

"I think I can do it if I take a big step and a bit of a jump at the same time. There's no obvious way round so I'd better get on with it."

Water trickled over brown stones eight feet under the gap. With my left foot forward as close to the edge as I dared to put it, I rocked my weight backwards and forwards from one leg to the other.

"Now!" I shouted.

Launching my weight forward, I shot the right leg out like a hurdler. At the same time the left leg provided a push and the right boot landed on the far side. It was more of a controlled topple than a jump. I had sufficient momentum to throw my body forward and the left foot reached the far side too.

"Good," Hans Balmer said. "Champagne!"

As we continued a rock crunched down the mountain a hundred feet from us. Like an under-inflated football it bounced in shallow arcs, and was soon out of sight. For several seconds we heard it thudding on. Now that we were descending, gravity was more in our favour, but could still cause a fall or send down an avalanche.

A few minutes later Hans Balmer shouted from behind.

"Achtung!"

I turned to see something flying through the air towards me. I ducked behind a rock and was showered by small particles of ice. The ice had smashed on the rock and the pieces were too small to do any harm. For an instant as they fell they had looked menacing. I think Hans Kaufmann thought I had fallen when I leapt behind the rock.

We carried on.

"When we reach your rucksack we will rest and have something to eat. Then we can go down to the hotel," Hans Kaufmann said.

"That will not be wise," I told him. "I think I should not climb much more today."

"We should not bivouac up here if we can get back to the hotel."

The last hour before we arrived at the boulder where we had left my rucksack was a wearying trudge. In the heat my stumps began to feel very painful. It was four o'clock so we had climbed for thirteen hours. That was the longest I had ever climbed and I could not expect the stumps to take much more punishment without serious damage. I estimated that it would take four to six hours to reach the hotel. To climb for such a length of time would far exceed my reasonable limits.

When we had rested for a few minutes Hans Kaufmann said, "Now we must go down."

"I think we should stay here," I objected.

"If it snows we could be in trouble," he added.

"It's a bit late to remember that it sometimes snows up here."

191

Hans Balmer picked up my rucksack and was busy tying it on the top of his own. The extra few pounds would not make much difference to him.

Certainly, if we went well below half-way we would be safer in the event of a storm. The weather was fine but it was possible it would change.

"I'll go on for an hour or two and see how I feel," I said.

Needless to say, I moved slowly, fatigue was partly responsible and I could not put my heart into a descent which I regarded as unnecessary and unwise. From experience I knew that once the stumps had had enough their condition would deteriorate rapidly.

The fourteenth hour of climbing went by. I moved like an unwilling slave. I could keep going, but wondered if I should.

"How heavy are you?" Hans Kaufmann asked.

I told him.

"If you become very tired we could carry you when it is dark," he said.

"No you bloody well won't!"

"No one would know."

"I would know."

Hans Balmer joined in, saying, "You are

very hard-headed. Just because you have no legs you don't want to be carried, but sometimes men who have whole legs have to be carried. Some people like to say they have bivouacked on many mountains."

"It doesn't take much sense to see that this is a special case. We knew I would have to bivouac."

"You have climbed down all right so far," Hans Kaufmann said.

There was no rhythm to my climbing: each movement had become a separate mental and physical effort in a disjointed labour.

The fifteenth hour passed—a whole, long hour of great exertion and failing concentration. We took a rest. Lying back on a rock, I tried to muster my thoughts. I had climbed to the summit and descended to a safe height to bivouac and it was not sensible to go on. I was worried about causing serious physical damage to my stumps. I vomited, through sheer overwork.

"Come on," Hans Balmer said after three or four minutes.

Hans Kaufmann tugged at the rope to get me to stand.

"Hang on a minute!" I said. "I want time to think."

Thoughts came slowly and were hard to grasp. Feelings flooded my mind: exhaustion, pain, elation, indecision, anxiety about my physical limits. I could have sat down at any time and refused to move, so why didn't I? The truth was that although I believed it was stupid to continue, half of me wanted to complete the climb in a day. It felt so wrong to go on for more than fifteen hours; I battled with my own better judgment. I would have liked half an hour in which to sort out my jumbled thoughts.

"Come on!" Hans Balmer said. "You can do it."

I stood and began to climb down again. The sixteenth hour crept by. By half past seven it was getting dark. We were at the top of the lowest snowfield. The two English mountaineers we had seen earlier passed by. Poor snow had forced them to give up not far from the summit, on the final snowfield, and I realised how lucky we had been. In the whole day they were the only climbers we saw.

"You can sleep in a good bed when you get to the hotel," Hans Kaufmann remarked to me.

"I could sleep in a good sleeping bag now if

you bandits would stop," I said. "Anyway, I want some of that champagne if we get down tonight."

"Of course," he said. He smiled. "You know, you will be happy if you climb the Eiger in one day."

"I hoped to climb the Eiger but I did not want to be a stupid sort of mountaineer. I would never have set out to climb it in one day."

On the descent of the snowfield my knee joints ached more and the flesh at the back of the knees was tender. That worried me because knees do not seem to put up well with bad treatment. I wondered how long I could go on without suffering serious effects from exhaustion and excessive exercise. One thought frequently entered my mind, that I was not cold. It was a good sign.

The seventeenth hour passed. After the first six hours of climbing I was, understandably, quite tired. Six more hours had taken me to what I considered to be the extreme of my reasonable limits. Five hours of discomfort and fatigue had followed and we still had to descend a long way over rock. We needed torches on the lower part of the snowfield and I did not relish descending the rock by torchlight. But I did not stage a sit-down strike. I knew if I insisted on bivouacking the guides would stay with me: they could not risk abandoning me on the mountain. I wondered why they were so keen to reach the hotel. Was the attraction the thought of proving the other guides wrong? All the time I wondered why I did not stop, and the only reason I could find was that I wanted to complete the route in one day. My cautious self had to be content that we were approaching safety. Obviously, determination and sense were not to be completely and simultaneously satisfied on this occasion.

I appreciated that it was a big mental strain for guides to undertake the responsibility of leading a disabled client on a long route. The pair with me were amongst the very small number of Grindelwald guides prepared to take the job on, and I was grateful to them.

Our torches probed through the darkness, seeking the way. It was not easy to find. Hans Balmer went ahead, searching for a route down the rock steps. He wandered to the left and right, finding the route and losing it every few minutes. I took advantage of every delay to rest. We meandered down for an hour, the eighteenth hour. I had passed through hardship into joy, then back deeper and deeper into hardship; but the joy was still complete.

Someone with a powerful torch left the hotel and came towards us. From a few hundred feet above them we could see that they were waving the torch around. It was Birgit and Barry, the English chef, swinging the torch about in greeting and encouragement. They signalled for several minutes before returning to the hotel. It was nice to know someone was thinking of us.

Every step down, every reach for a handhold, was like the movememt of someone who has just woken in the middle of the night. My feet might have been made of lead, not aluminium.

The nineteenth hour came to an end. Slowly, we neared the lights of the Eiger Glacier station. At last we reached the track through the glacial moraine. Nearly there. We passed by the railway lines and overhead cables, the houses and huts. We were a few yards from the hotel when I saw a table supporting glasses and bottles of champagne. A dozen or fifteen people waited to welcome us. As we reached the hotel entrance the television crew started to film. Suddenly it came to me that I was feeling cold. It was a strange sort of feeling which I could not understand. It was like nothing I had felt before. Then I put my hand down and found that there was no seat at all left in my trousers! From then on I made sure I was facing the camera.

The time was half past ten and the climb had lasted nineteen and a half hours.

"You look well for someone who's been up there all day," said Bruno, the manager of the Jungfraujoch self-service restaurant.

"Well done," Richard said with great enthusiasm. "We wish we had been with you."

Everyone seemed thrilled. Herby started pouring champagne. Richard conducted another interview, then we had a celebration meal and wine. While several people drank, laughed and talked loudly in the restaurant I fell asleep sitting upright. It was a sleep brought on by contentment more than exhaustion.

The next day I heard from Richard that Hans Kaufmann had said in advance that he had no intention of bivouacking unless it was absolutely necessary. I was angry about that, but the guides had carried out the job and I liked the pair of rogues. And I could have insisted on stopping. By carrying on I had been taught something new about my limits: sense was likely to stop me long before fatigue.

Frau Sommer arranged a champagne breakfast for the morning after the climb. Frau Sommer, Bruno, the guides, Barry and I sat on the hotel balcony for a meal of eggs and bacon, assorted meats and pickles, tea and champagne. The next day I went to Berne for a radio recording, and a Scotsman at the studio provided more champagne. I flew home the same day and at our local pub there was more champagne as soon as Judy and I walked through the doorway. "Congratulations on your feat," someone said, and from somebody else came, "He hasn't got any". For a few days life revolved around newspapers, radio and television broadcasts, and celebrations with friends. Then it all went back to normal.

Another ambition was behind me, and I strongly wished to rid myself of big ambitions for they would not let me rest until I put them quiet by achieving them. I wanted to go out and climb simply for enjoyment, without any pressing ambitions getting in the way. Now there were no urgent goals, and that was pleasing for a while.

7

"WHERE shall we go next summer, Norm?" Dave asked one winter afternoon. "Alps again?"

"I've no plans yet."

We were climbing with Len in the Taff's Well Quarry, near Dave's South Wales home.

"I want to do the Weisshorn next year," Len said. "I've wanted to climb the Weisshorn for years."

"Zermatt then," Dave remarked. "All right with you, Norm?"

"Fine. There's a route I'd thought about on a peak near Saas Fee and we can get there easily from Zermatt."

"Zermatt it is then," Dave announced.

So it was decided. The idea was suggested and adopted without question. Len had seen the Weisshorn years before and ever since had wanted to climb the mountain. The three of us had assumed we would climb together, so Zermatt it would be. What a contrast it was to the previous three years when I had burned to achieve certain objectives. 1973

200

promised to bring a more relaxed summer.

That same day we climbed a 240-foot route up the quarry wall. The climb, called Pine Tree, was graded Very Difficult. Though not a very interesting climb, it was an important event because the experience led me to adopt two new pieces of equipment which were to cause many bewildered and disapproving looks when I used them—knee pads.

Len led the first pitch, eighty feet up a buttress, now and then passing tiny, gaping rock mouths full of crystal teeth. The second pitch rose leftward up a wide crack to a belay at a pine tree. The smooth rock demanded flexible foot movement which I could not manage, but I grovelled somehow. A rising rightwards traverse followed, then Dave took the lead. He called down to me.

"You're going to enjoy the last bit." He grinned and pointed upwards. "Over that nose. It's steep and part of it overhangs so you can't see where your feet are as you go over the top."

"That means I won't be able to see if they are on the holds and I won't be able to feel if they are on either."

"And I'll tell you something else," he went on. He bore a resemblance to a sadist who has been given a whip for his birthday. "There aren't any handholds worth talking about. It's all done with the feet!"

As he mounted the nose his toes stayed on the little ledges which his eyes could not see. The nose was only a few feet high but it was steep. The fact that it was a couple of hundred feet made it look a bit more difficult. Technically, though, it was easy for a climber with feet.

"I'll give it a try now, Dave."

The grinning Parsons peered down from his perch.

"O.K."

Pulling up with both hands I raised my right leg. The shin clattered against the rock with a sound like a pewter jug. The toe was on a smallish hold. Or was it? I couldn't tell because it was out of sight. By leaning out it was possible to look down and reassure myself. Eyes ran over the rock to pick out holds. Alternately my hands left their meagre holds to scour the rock. Having explored and found nothing, they returned to where they had been. Several times they went out and returned disappointed. The right boot slipped a little.

"I think my boot's off the rock."

"Heh! Heh!"

"Grotty holds."

The rounded smooth handholds helped to keep me up only as long as I could maintain great pressure on them through fingers and thumbs. If the grip relaxed the hands began to slide off. Pulling upon the poor handholds, I tried to find friction on the rock with my boots. They slipped quite often. I rose a little farther, relying mostly on the pull of my arms.

Suddenly an idea flashed through my mind—knee pads! With knee pads it would be possible to gain a little extra friction in some circumstances and this would help to make up for the friction lost through being unable to angle my feet to advantage on the rock. And it would be possible to see where I was putting the pads.

The idea was not much assistance at the time. I clung on and got to within a few feet of Dave. My hands reached up and curled over holds which hardly existed. I hung there and tried to raise my boots but they slipped. My thighs trembled with the effort.

"Blasted rock!" I hissed. "Blasted rock!"

It was only Very Difficult, but it looked as if it might beat me. Fingers ached and arms trembled with the strain. Gradually my fingers began to straighten, releasing the holds. As strength ebbed I looked at them and told them to arch over the rock but slowly they continued to straighten. My feet were slipping. I thought I was going to fall.

"I'm going Dave!"

He stood at the top, waiting to hold me if I fell. I once asked him whether he worried about the consequences if I fell while climbing with him. His reply, "Not as long as you don't fall on me, you bugger," contrasted with the real concern he showed for my safety.

"I'm going!" I said again.

"Fight, you sod!"

"I'm going!"

The rope was tight.

"Fight!"

"I'm going . . . up!"

I could hardly believe it, but I pulled with my arms and scrabbled with feet and knees and did go up, to crawl up to Dave. The energy born of desperation lasted long enough to get me that far, and no farther. I slumped on the ground at his feet.

"That was a mess," I remarked.

"Amazing!" Dave said. "Amazing! That's

the first time I've ever seen anybody climb solely on handholds where there aren't any handholds! Amazing!"

"Hardly what you would call poetry in motion."

At least that ungraceful performance brought about the idea of using knee pads. Climbers do not normally kneel on rock, and I had usually avoided doing so. Once you rest on a knee it can put you off balance and it may be difficult to get a foot back on the rock, and if the knee slips it can be easily injured. But if I wore rubber knee pads they would protect the knees and give added friction.

Pieces of a rubber car mat and four dog collars were soon turned into two strap-on pads. Dave and I climbed a short, easy route on a limestone sea cliff.

"You really bombed up that," Dave said. "Three times as fast as usual."

We looked around for a harder route, and journeyed to Churchill Rocks, where I had climbed before. I usually settled on little-known outcrops because I did not like having many people around. This was for two reasons: firstly, I was slow and got in the way on busy routes, and secondly, I disliked having an audience to witness my ungainly progress. On the big slab of limestone at Churchill Rocks I had climbed the first Severe route I ever managed a couple of years before. Another route beckoned this time, the Left Hand route, a hundred and ten feet long. It ran up the slab roughly parallel to the route climbed on the previous visit, and it was graded one of the easier climbs in the Severe grade (Mild Severe or Just Severe). There was nothing outstanding about the climb, which was not very steep but was quite hard because of a lack of holds. In places knobs of rock as big as coat buttons were the biggest that could be found, and sometimes even holds like these were absent.

Dave went up an easy way, found a tree belay and called to me to climb. I started. A couple of small footholds, a pair of thin cracks which accommodated a few fingertips, occasional patches of pink, knobbly, friendly rock, then more bare, smooth, grey rock. Grunt, grasp, growl. Fifteen feet up. Twenty feet. Minutes crept by. The finger strain at times was tremendous.

"I'm letting the rope stay slack so you're not helped by the tension, Norm."

Where possible I used the footholds, and quite often put a knee on the rock for extra friction. Twenty minutes of clutching at tiny holds put me about half-way up. The holds did not improve and my grunting increased until I sounded like a ring full of wrestlers. Seventy feet up: there was a band of rock, two yards high, looking like concrete. Not a hold to be seen, but somehow I scrabbled up, slipping a little now and then but gaining height in the end.

"Superb!" Dave shouted in encouragement.

There was more concrete-like rock, and once I slipped and might have gone on slipping had it not been for the rope. A small, deep hole made a welcome handhold and, later, a foothold. At no time was it easy, but soon I knew I was winning. The smooth rock gave way to a shattered area of grassy cracks, and I was up.

"Would never have managed without the pads," I told Dave.

He abseiled down the slab and was back up the route in five or six minutes. I was constantly aware that where I moved with great difficulty, the others went with ease. But no one gained more pleasure from the rock than I. No one.

"Well, you've done a couple of Severes and you know you can do some more."

"I often wonder how I would manage on a climb like that if I had legs."

"Yes. You must miss them."

"I was very attached to them."

"Your jokes get worse."

The plans for the summer trip took shape. Len and Dave and a few other members of the club would go to Zermatt in August. The only definite target was Len's, the Weisshorn.

Over the few months preceding the summer trip, Dave and I climbed together quite often. I also got in some practice at artificial climbing, though banging in pitons did not appeal to me as much as the "free" climbing I had done. One professional instructor, Terry Tullis, gave me a lesson for nothing.

"I injured my leg badly a couple of years ago," he said. "I lay in hospital wondering if they would have to amputate. Then I read about you doing your walk from John o' Groats to Land's End and that made me feel if they had to it would not be so bad. I didn't lose my leg after all but I was worried for a while. I feel like I'm repaying you."

I went to several sandstone outcrops near

London with different climbers and each time came away frustrated with the rock, which just did not suit me because the climbs often required flexible ankle movements. I walked and scrambled in the Brecon Beacons, North Wales and the Lake District, and paid particular attention to abseil practice because I found it difficult in some circumstances. Abseiling has led to many fatal accidents, particularly when the anchor at which the rope has been attached has given way or the rope has slipped from the anchor.

In April 1973 came the annual club jaunt to Cornwall. It was delightful to be back on the granite cliffs of my climbing initiation, but this was not an occasion confined to climbing; a football match on the beach, sing-songs in the First and Last Inn, and walks among the lesser celandines, primroses, violets and blazes of gorse were as much a part of the holiday as the rock. Forty club members turned up to camp in a field a mile or two from Land's End, and several had a fine time without climbing at all.

I watched Dave on one climb on rock which was wet with rain.

"This must be at least Severe, and it's wet," he called down. "It's 'ard."

"I know," his wife said. "I can tell—his voice has gone up an octave."

One interesting climb proved the usefulness of the knee pads. We were at Chair Ladder, a cliff not far from Land's End.

"Let's do Terrier's Tooth," Dave suggested. "It's a V. Diff."

There were some other climbers on the first pitch so we took an alternative, easier way to start. The pads helped a great deal on that pitch.

"I found a kneesy way to do that," I said, and Dave groaned and threatened to throw me in the sea.

The finish of the climb was quite spectacular. From an exposed position a hundred feet above the sea a slab was mounted by jamming a hand in a crack and pulling up. The route terminated on a rock pinnacle and from an airy seat we sat and watched the sun sink imperceptibly towards a calm, flat sea. The enjoyment lay as much in looking back as in taking part.

"How about doing the Matterhorn in the summer?" Dave asked.

"I've thought about it. I'm not too sure. The normal route is crowded. I like quieter routes. But I'm tempted."

"It'll be a great summer anyway," he said. "It's nice to look forward."

We arrived in ones and twos at the Zermatt camp-site, about 5,000 feet (1,600 metres) above sea level. Dave was bleary-eyed after an all night journey standing in the crowded corridor of a train from Austria. Len and two other club members, Don Hillman and John Hodgkins, turned up soon after, and finally came Adrian and Alan. Two hundred yards from the tents was a landing pad which helicopters roared up several times a day, lifting provisions and people in minutes from the valley to huts on high peaks all around. Mountains of twelve and thirteen thousand feet were a common sight on both sides of the valley.

"Out of all these peaks it's always the Thing that stands out," Dave said. The Thing was the Matterhorn. Steep on all sides and wildly beautiful, the remarkable pyramid demanded attention and it was easy to see why it tempted climbers to the top.

Five of us decided to go up to the Rothorn hut and climb a peak or two from there. The hut, at 10,500 feet (3,177 metres) is about five hours walk from Zermatt along a well-beaten trail. As it would be the first alpine trek of the season I reckoned it would take me near eight hours. In the heat of the day this would not be at all pleasant so I set out ahead of the others in the cool of the early evening.

Up the steep Trift Gorge, over a sturdy wooden bridge, through a forest, never far from the stream which found its way noisily down the middle of the gorge. As shadows lengthened and the gorge grew cool, hikers thinned out; still in any stretch of half a mile at least a dozen people would pass, heading down the trail to their dinners in Zermatt. The track left the forest. Trees were replaced by short vegetation which clung close to the ground in a carpet which successfully survived the harsh environment.

Two men called from a hundred yards farther along the trail and pointed up the steep mountainside to my right. Leaping up with graceful strides were two chamois, moving with bounds which looked as near to effortless as you could imagine. I've read that they can jump more than a dozen feet in the air.

Two and a half hours out of the valley, the abandoned Trift Hotel loomed on the right of the track. There was no one in sight on the trail, above or below, and the decaying building had an eerie look about it in its lonely mountain setting at 7,500 feet (2,337 metres). Deserted, neglected, disused, unwanted, the building had been robbed of any significance to mountaineers by the more recently built and higher Rothorn hut.

Darkness was less than an hour away. Rotting floorboards and stinking debris left by passing tourists made it preferable to sleep outside the hotel. In a sleeping bag I slept heavily under the brilliant stars. It was worth going to the Rothorn hut just to see that night and the beautiful sunrise the next day.

Morning started in bright sunshine with a slow walk along grassy moraines to a stony plateau. A cold stream fed by melting ice farther up the mountainside broadened to form a small, shallow lake trapped in an undulation of the plateau.

I had been walking for an hour when a sudden, piercing whistle startled me. On a rock a few yards away stood a marmot, a stocky, short-legged, squirrel-like inhabitant of the alps. They grew up to two feet long, but this one was shorter. It remained on all fours for several seconds, then darted away behind the rock. The whistle I had heard was the marmot's alarm signal, a signal which has saved many a chamois from an approaching hunter.

The long haul began up the crest of a lateral moraine; this type of moraine is a pile of rubble forced up along the edge of a glacier by the tremendous force of that glacier. In this case the Trift Glacier had done the work with its gigantic ice tongue.

It grew hot. I rested frequently and tried to pick out my companions on their way up. Several people passed by, puffing, but always taking the trouble to mutter a word of greeting. Eight thousand feet, nine thousand, ten thousand. The altitude had a considerable effect. There was no point in rushing so I strolled on for six hours and sat beside a stream near a small snowfield to wait for the others. The Rothorn hut was only ten minutes' walk away. I dozed in the sun several times, and felt rather pleased with myself because I had for the first time made a long hut walk from the valley instead of using mechanical transport.

I went on to the hut and my four friends straggled up the trail an hour later. They decided to climb the Trifthorn the next day. A peak of a little over 12,000 feet (3,728 metres), it was a fairly easy training climb. I stuck to the usual rule of not doing too much too soon and opted out, though I was not sure whether this was through sense or sloth.

The others got up early, at half past three, and spent a few pleasant hours going up and down the Trifthorn, without incident.

Four o'clock the next day saw us all, apart from Len, tramping over crusty snow up the Trift Glacier. John and Don were ahead by a few minutes. For a while Dave wore a head-torch, but it was soon daylight.

"Crevasse there," he warned as he stepped over a gaping slit in the glacier. "And another."

Many times we made a big step across a crevasse. I knew several people who had fallen in crevasses, but had never done so myself. Even so, it was one of the mountain dangers of which I was extremely aware. Gingerly, we went on our way.

We picked our way across an ice slope of twenty degrees or less. The sun rose to shed pink light on the mountains.

"Look at that panorama!" Dave said every few minutes. Neither he nor I could resist the temptation to stop many times and absorb the scenery with our eyes.

The target was the Wellenkuppe, 12,800

feet high (3,903 metres). The route was quite easy and relatively short.

We curved to the left up the glacier, across more crevasses, and the snow steepened—time for crampons. Mounting a broad, glistening shoulder of snow, from which the route swept sharply to the right, we kept close to but a little below a sharp rock ridge. This was the sort of place where helmets were a wise precaution. And sure enough, a few minutes after we had put our helmets on, down came a nasty shower of stones. They bounced past us a few yards away.

Rock gave way to snow, and snow to rock. With crampons removed, we climbed over easy rock which in most places was sound and rarely steeper than forty-five degrees. One short exception, a few degrees from the vertical, was loose and unpleasant. An impressive slab section was climbed for two hundred feet on firm, dry rock with abundant holds.

"Can't be far now," Dave remarked as we neared the top of the slab. He was right. The rock finished and stretching up to the summit was a gently rising snow crest, and in fifteen minutes or less we joined Don and John on the broad snow top. They had been waiting a long time for us.

From there we could see other people going farther, to the Obergabelhorn. As we were newly arrived in the Alps I was not so ambitious. It was sufficient to make a leisurely ascent of the Wellenkuppe.

John and Don were cold through waiting and started back down. In a few minutes we followed down the snow, down the slab in two pitches of a hundred feet or so. On the second pitch I was facing outwards with my hands, bottom and boots on the rock. This was the quickest and easiest way to descend in the circumstances. A crack running parallel to our direction of travel was just wide enough to jam a boot in to give a firm hold. Unfortunately it proved to be too firm and the boot stuck fast. Pulling was no good. I thought about having to leave behind a boot, complete with foot and leg, to puzzle future generations of alpinists. But no, if tugging failed I could unlace the boot and pull the foot out, then the leather would not be jammed tight. I pulled the leg with both hands to no avail, so began to kick the wedged boot with the other. In a few seconds it was free. Have to watch that in future, I thought.

When we reached the glacier I again encountered the old adversary, soft snow. Dave strode along with relative ease while I floundered. My boots sank deep, seeming unwilling to go on. In similar circumstances Geoffrey Winthrop Young, a one-legged mountaineer, thought, "the Trift glacier would at this hour be for me impassable, and exceedingly dangerous, with snow-covered crevasses under broiling sunshine".

Each time I passed over a crevasse I warned Dave to look out for it. The icy, green depths looked menacing, but the real danger lay in the depths we could not see as we trod the soft mantle. The afternoon sun beat down with unpleasant fierceness.

"This is murder," I told Dave.

"Looks like the only solution will be skis or snow-shoes. Best to stick to rock until you have some."

"I've been avoiding them because it will mean humping around extra gear, but it looks like the only way."

Every so often I went on a climb which led to the solution of a problem. The ski basket on the end of an ice-axe, knee pads, snow-shoes: these and other aids made a great difference, and it was worth going on the

Wellenkuppe just to reach the decision in favour of using snow-shoes.

Bootprints of previous parties showed the route, but there was no way of knowing that snow which had held an hour before would now support the weight of a man. Hardness had deserted the snow and would only return with the night. A prod with an ice-axe here and there helped to confirm that the snow was thick.

Progress was slow, but eventually we reached the comfort of firm rock near the hut. It had taken nearly five hours to climb up and almost as long to descend. Slow going.

"That was a grand day," Dave said. "No epics, time to look around. Very pleasant."

By the time I arrived back at the camp-site the next day, the greater part of a week had elapsed since arriving in Zermatt. Including treks to and from huts, an occasional rest day, and allowing for the weather, my lack of mobility meant that I could expect to climb only three or four peaks in a holiday of three weeks. The descent from the Rothorn hut which my companions had tacked on to the end of a day's climbing had been for me four and a half very hot hours, and it was preferable to take yet another unwanted day of idleness to help some small abrasions on my stumps to heal. Once more I paid for an ascent with pain. I knew the lesson so well: when the stumps became damaged, a day of relaxation prevented them from deteriorating further. Even though they would not actually heal in twenty-four hours, after that period of inactivity a moderately long climb would not cause much further harm. Time and time again this had proved true.

We witnessed a very sad scene. Next to ours stood two tiny tents, temporary homes for four young Japanese men. We didn't see much of them because they spent most of their time climbing. One afternoon word filtered down to the valley that two Japanese had fallen to their deaths on the normal route on the Matterhorn. It did not occur to us that it might be two of the men from the neighbouring tents because there were hordes of Japanese climbers in the Alps. But on the morning following the announcement of the accident two of the men turned up, obviously shocked, to pack up both tents and all the equipment. They did so quietly and one sight really brought home the sadness of the occasion—when the two small men left the campsite each was burdened with two large rucksacks, one tied on top of the other.

Most of our group chose to climb the Breithorn next. This is very easy by the normal route but it is snow all the way. The snow was in poor condition and had been so for many days because of high temperatures; some people reported that the snow on that route was soft even early in the morning.

"You coming, Norm?" someone asked.

"No thanks. I'll stick to the rock until the temperature goes down a bit."

"Wish I had legs like yours," Dave said. "I wouldn't have to climb so much with an excuse like that."

Adrian, Alan and I headed up the Ober Rothorn, which is just over 11,200 feet (3,415 metres). It was just a walk, during which Adrian repeatedly popped up on boulders, like the marmot on the way to the Rothorn hut. Unlike the marmot he kept yodelling, "And your old lady too."

Close to the top we passed a lady who had stopped for a rest. As I went by she said, helpfully, "You should put your feet like this," and demonstrated how to place them.

"I'd like to if I had any," was all I could think of saying at the time, and then I spent a while chatting to assure her that there was no need to be embarrassed.

It reminded me of something which happened at Jungfraujoch a couple of years earlier. Close to the hotel was a small, snowy plateau which was reached by a gently sloping snow path. On day I was walking up the path when I heard an American man say to two women with him, "That guy must know what he's doing because he's wearing the right boots and clothes. See how he walks on his toes? Now that's the way to do it. Come on, let's go!"

Within seconds there was a tremendous smack as he hit the snow and the last I saw of him he was being helped back to the hotel by his companions.

The summit of the Ober Rothorn was distinct but heavily eroded by human presence. The soft rock had been broken down to dust. We did not stay long before heading down.

Back at the camp-site Dave was preparing a chicken curry. He was pleased at having been able to purchase very cheaply a bag full of bits of chicken. When he came to tip the bits in a pan they turned out to be mostly from the very back ends of the birds. Considering that his surname is Parsons, it was appropriate.

Later on he told me about the Breithorn.

"You were right not to go up with us. It's dead easy but the snow's soft. Like walking on porridge. Don and I went up Monte Rosa and it was the same."

"I'll stick mostly to rock then."

"How about the Thing? That's mostly rock. Better than festering down here."

"I've mixed feelings, but I think I'd like to go."

"It's a fantastic shape. Pity to miss the chance while you're here. We could climb part way and see how it goes."

"As far as the Solvay hut, perhaps."

Len, John and Don went off to the Weisshorn, while Adrian and Alan picked the Allalinhorn.

The Belvedere Hotel on the Hörnli ridge of the Matterhorn was much improved since my previous visit and the kitchen, particularly, was no longer filthy. We stayed in the hut next door and were away by half past three the next morning, along with about sixty other alpinists.

The moon was just bright enough to manage without a torch although most people wore head torches. We followed a long line of lights up a rocky path. A fixed rope of twenty feet hung down the first bit of climbable rock and everyone went up quickly, hand over hand, with feet walking up. Without that rope there would have been a bottleneck close to the hut.

An easy track climbed and dipped, and several lights in front veered a little to the right into dark shadow. The track steepened. Everyone else continued to walk upright but I found it easier to scramble than to walk in some places.

"Not like that!"

The voice from behind me spoke in German. The leader of a party of three was talking to me. My knowledge of German was poor, but I did my best to explain my unconventional technique.

"I must. I have no legs," I said. At least, that's what I thought I said.

The man made no reply and headed away up the mountain with great speed. No wonder! A friend explained to me later that what I actually said was, "I must. I have no bees."

We followed the lights up a crumbly rock face, nearly vertical in places but very easy.

At the top a party of three seemed to be having trouble. We had to wait quite a long time while the leader descended into darkness over a cliff. In a minute there was a sound of clattering rock from his direction, a sound which recurred several times in the next few minutes. The leader called up; he sounded anxious. The man feeding the rope down to him found a spike of rock and passed the rope around it.

"I don't remember this bit," Dave remarked. He had been on the route before, once when he climbed up and down that way and once when descending after climbing the Zmutt ridge of the mountain.

Time crept by and the leader's rope was fed out slowly.

"Wrong way," Dave said. "Must be. There's nothing difficult around this part of the route."

"Might as well go down the bit we've come up then."

"Yes."

We retraced our way down the rock face. As the light improved we saw that we had been on the top of a rock tower which stuck up on the ridge. In all we must have wasted a large part of an hour by following the wrong people. They passed us again an hour later. We pressed on over slopes of broken rock.

"What a heap of rubbish," Dave remarked. At close quarters the mountain lost much of its beauty.

People above were dislodging lots of stones and in the half-light it was not easy to see them coming. We were worried, with good reason as it happened. As one shower of Mother Nature's cannonballs bounced down we froze, ready to duck or dodge. The stones thudded down to our right and stopped not far below as they hit a large ledge. A minute or two later another rock barrage began to fall from three hundred feet above. They came nearer and nearer but we could not see them. Judging from the noise it gradually became more and more evident that they were coming our way. We pressed ourselves against the rock. Clunk, clunk, clunk. Fist-sized stones sped by and there was a loud thump on my helmet. It was probably a glancing blow because the helmet was not split.

"Christ!" my companion muttered.

"You all right, Dave?"

He was about four yards away.

"Yes. They missed me. You all right?"

"Yes. Got a smack on the helmet. I think one hit my ice-axe too."

The axe was passed through a shoulder strap of my rucksack, between the rucksack and my back. On this occasion the axe had a wooden shaft, and when I came to examine it in daylight there was a chip of wood missing. I was lucky not to have been struck on the back of the neck.

"What a heap of rubbish!" Dave said again.

Snow patches were only a few square yards in area. The rock was poor in many places.

Difficulty in route-finding slowed us. It was not that we went the wrong way often, but time was lost as we talked over which way looked best. We lacked the confidence of being sure we were on the route. Instead of thrusting ahead, as one can on some obvious routes, we had to pick the way. Added to this I did not feel well and wondered if the altitude was having an effect.

Other parties had route-finding problems and after four hours' climbing several people were only a few minutes ahead. A man with a bandaged head descended with two companions.

Nowhere was the rock climbing above

Moderate standard. In six hours we were at the Solvay hut, 13,120 feet (4,000 metres). That was a very long time—four hours would have been satisfactory for me.

The hut was perched right on the sharp ridge. Five or six disconsolate people hung around, waiting for friends who had carried on. Most were tired, probably because of the altitude, and one had injured his knee in a fall. He felt that he would be unable to descend so a message was taken to the Hörnli hut to summon a helicopter. We made some soup, and while the three of us drank it the injured man told us his injury resulted from a fall of about twenty feet. He was an engineer, originally from Czechoslovakia but living in Switzerland.

"What shall we do tomorrow?" Dave asked me. "To tell the truth, I'm not too happy to go on when there are only two of us."

"I was thinking about that. We usually would have someone else on a route like this. Not only that, I'm not feeling too good."

"That explains why you almost bit my head off a couple of times."

"I'm not my usual charming, even modest self."

"So we'd better go down tomorrow?"

"I think so. Anyway, this has been a good reconnaissance."

"Yes. You wouldn't have any trouble with the rest of the route."

All afternoon, climbers descended in twos, threes and fours. Intermittently, mist covered the Hörnli ridge.

Shortly after six o'clock we heard the distant noise of a helicopter. Dave and I stood outside the hut on the narrow stone platform which ran along its front like a pavement. The platform stretched the full length of the front of the hut, about sixteen feet, and was just wide enough for people to pass each other over a big drop. This was the only way past the hut, and the platform was used by all people ascending and descending. The helicopter roared up the valley until it was above, then dropped slowly to hover within thirty feet of the hut roof. What a racket! A man appeared at a door in the side of the machine and stepping out, he dangled on a cable.

"Sod that for a job," Dave said.

The man was lowered quickly to the level of the platform, but a few feet away. He hung there, spinning slowly in space far above the rock.

"He can keep his job," Dave said.

The helicopter manoeuvred a little, bringing the man to within something more than a yard of the platform with his feet at the same level. He continued to spin slowly and swayed gently from side to side. As he turned he extended an arm in my direction to be pulled into the platform. I leaned forward to grasp his hand and felt Dave grip my jacket at waist level from behind. I pulled the rescuer in and he released himself from the cable. The helicopter soared away.

"Where is the man?" the rescuer asked.

"Inside," we told him.

The rescuer fitted a harness on the casualty.

"Do you do this often?" Dave asked.

"Yes,"

"You can keep your job."

The rescuer spoke into a small radio and when the helicopter returned the injured man was hooked on to the cable and winched up. The rescuer followed shortly after.

At seven o'clock that evening people were still descending, in failing light, and several stayed at the Solvay hut. I was surprised at how long it took them—in fifteen hours they had been unable to complete the route, up and down. Navigation seemed to be the chief problem.

At six a.m. the next day we abseiled down a couple of steep pitches and climbed down the mountain.

"I'm still feeling a bit ill," I told Dave as we headed back to the camp-site. "It's a good job we didn't go up."

Next day I had a sore throat and 'flu-like symptoms. The holiday came to an end.

Len, Don and John had turned back on the Weisshorn for a number of reasons, including lack of sleep the night before, so Len's ambition was unrealised. I failed to climb the Thing and as it was a rubbishy route I was not disappointed. Or was I? My mind kept turning up the memory of a small, almost insignificant event which happened on the trail down from the mountain. Dave had gone ahead to get some drinks at Schwarzee. Turning to look at the Matterhorn I said, "One day, I will climb you, you shapely heap."

It was hard to believe that the words came from my mouth. Was I really talking to a mountain?

"One day I will climb you," I insisted.

It was strange. I had felt little ambition to stand on the summit, but it was as if the mountain had control and could make me want to climb. Where was my former indifference about that peak? It was gone for sure, for ever.

An outstanding mountaineer with an above-knee amputation, Geoffrey Winthrop Young, climbed the Matterhorn many years ago. He made several one-legged ascents including Monte Rosa, Grépon and Rothorn, and it was with remarkable spirit that he kept coming back for more. He gave up climbing after a fall of eighty feet which left him suspended on the rope beneath an overhang. He was fortunate to escape with minor injuries.

When I got home from Switzerland I read, in the *Matterhorn Centenary* by Sir Arnold Lunn, ". . . he was the first, and so far the only mountaineer to have climbed the Matterhorn after losing a leg".

These words seemed like a challenge. I would have to go back.

8

CLIMBING once more had an influence on the path my life took. The mountains had given me much pleasure and I wondered how many other disabled people took part in outdoor pursuits. There was a lack of information available, and after a talk with Lady Hamilton, Chairman of the Disabled Living Foundation, I was given the job of compiling a guide on outdoor pursuits for disabled people.

Although I was strongly in favour of competitive sports for disabled people, I felt that the emphasis had been so much on that side that non-competitive activities had been neglected, partly because of the often unfounded assumptions on the part of some organisers of sports for disabled people that such activities were beyond the abilities of the people they dealt with. There was a tendency to expect disabled people to take part only in a limited number of sports and mostly in a segregated situation. Total integration within the community was clearly not always possible but it did seem desirable to lean towards integration wherever this was realistic. With very few exceptions, only the more obvious and easiest sports had been tackled on a large scale; the most notable exception was the Riding for the Disabled Association, which brought riding to thousands of disabled young people and adults.

For advice I turned mostly to Miss K. Evans of the Disabled Living Foundation and Miss Elizabeth Dendy of the Sports Council, both of whom had an excellent knowledge of what was going on in the world of sport for disabled people. Soon information was coming in from all over the country and abroad. I came across isolated examples of activities which had been found suitable for many people with a variety of physical handicaps. For some (but not all) in wheelchairs the possibilities included camping, rowing, angling, sub-aqua diving, sailing, canoeing, gliding, shooting and riding, as well as field studies. Particularly with powered wheelchairs the potential of some nature trails was obvious, and hides at a few bird sanctuaries had been made accessible to wheelchairs. As passengers, there were chances for the more severely handicapped in, for example, boats, gliders, sand yachts and horse-drawn vehicles. For some disabled people who could walk (again, not for all) there was in addition rambling, cycling, skiing, water-skiing, climbing and caving.

Since becoming involved in compiling *Outdoor Pursuits for Disabled People* I have noticed a definite increase in concern for the subject in the media and within interested organisations, and I was pleased to be involved in various ways in several of these developments. The Spastics Society decided to build an adventure and field studies centre in Cornwall; at least five outdoor pursuits centres ran courses for disabled people; the Sports Council set up a steering committee concerned with water sports for disabled adults and children, and that committee published a book on angling, rowing, sailing, canoeing, sub-aqua diving and water-skiing; increasingly, mentally handicapped people were accepted at outdoor centres; an organisation for disabled skiers was formed; sailing schools took more disabled pupils; a course was run especially to investigate the safe limits in sub-aqua diving for paraplegics and amputees; experiments were carried out in what types of lifejackets, buoyancy aids and protective clothing best suited physically handicapped sailors and canoeists; a guide was compiled to access for those in wheelchairs or with walking difficulties, in about fifty nature reserves; and the outdoor pursuits guide was published. As months went by it was encouraging to see a move towards the ideal of as many sports as possible being made available to people with all handicaps. Always there was the proviso that the activity should be suitable from a medical and safety point of view, although most outdoor pursuits could never be completely free of risk. But at least the debate on safety and medical aspects was begun, rather than faint-heartedly avoided, as in the past.

One exciting development was a week-long course organised by Miss Dendy at Plas y Brenin, the National Mountaineering Centre in Snowdonia. Twelve young people between the ages of fourteen and eighteen years, plus seven disabled adults, joined in to determine what could be achieved, to identify problems and where possible to find solutions. Two physiotherapists and a doctor attended. The young people were accompanied by staff who knew them from their school or college. Eight of the participants normally used wheelchairs, the majority for most or all of the day. Handicaps included spina bifida, cerebral palsy (people with this handicap are commonly known as spastics), congenital deformity of one arm, paraplegia, multiple sclerosis, polio, rheumatism and arthritis, single and double leg amputation, and asthma. I shall never forget the experience.

There was clearly a feeling of nervousness amongst the participants who assembled on the first evening.

"I nearly didn't come," said Sally, a physiotherapist in her thirties. Sally had had multiple sclerosis for five years. "I don't think I'll be able to join in any activities."

She was in for a surprise.

The next morning those who could manage, including three with cerebral palsy, went hill walking. Meanwhile, seven people in wheelchairs headed for the swimming pool to practise canoe capsize drills. Having seen a demonstration of canoeing by girls from a school for handicapped children in Hampshire, I was expecting at least a few of our group to find the sport suitable. By the afternoon all but one had progressed to canoeing on a small lake.

Sally's determination soon showed and by

the end of the week she had canoed the Menai Strait and a few miles on a trip around an island off Anglesey. For someone who could manage only short distances on crutches, the sport gave a marvellous freedom of movement in wild places. One of the assistant instructors who helped Sally towards this discovery was himself disabled through polio and walked with considerable difficulty. Canoeing held obvious potential for many of the nineteen people on the course, both for those who excelled and for others who could paddle only relatively short distances in situations carefully chosen by an instructor, after medical considerations had been properly taken into account. It cannot be over-emphasised that each prospective participant had to be treated as an individual.

Skiing and ski-bobbing came next, on the steep artificial slope at the centre. Obviously, skiing was restricted to those who could stand, and the majority of them progressed at about the rate of able-bodied learners. Most noticeable on the slope were two very experienced one-legged skiers who performed with great skill. The instructor himself suffered from a mobility handicap, arthritis of the hips. The weather turned very bad: wind, rain and then big, stinging hails, in June. But no one went in and when the hails ceased the skiing was resumed.

Ski-bobs look rather like bicycle frames with skis in the place of wheels. Several of us were amazed at how easy the bobs were to ride, and were soon skimming down the slope from top to bottom. Sally was once more the star turn, and you can imagine the thrill for a former skier to find that she might still be able to glide down mountain slopes un-assisted. People who could not manage on their own were taken as passengers by the in-structors. Once more we had a disabled in-structor, with one leg, to show us the way.

The next ski slope activity was suitable for nearly everyone—tobogganing. Young and old alike zoomed down the incline, and some who could not walk crawled back for more. We concluded that good hand grips were essential on any toboggan for use by people with a variety of handicaps.

Next day in the pool a group started snorkelling, while others practised canoe rescues. At the same time one boy went angl-ing. The week was too short: a visit to a slate mine, skiing on a seven hundred metre cross-country track, swimming, riding in the rescue boat, rock climbing, rowing and sailing were crammed in. One of the instructors, Ken Roberts, had qualified as an instructor after becoming paraplegic in an accident. As chairman of the water sports committee he gave up a great deal of his spare time and did much to promote several water sports for disabled people, particularly by helping on sailing courses.

For several young people the highlight at the end of the course was a trip on the railway up Snowdon, the mountain they had heard so much about. As we waited to buy tickets the manager of the railway noticed our group and let us travel free. Then at the top station the guard helped to carry one boy fifty yards or so over the rough path to the summit. One cerebrally palsied boy who could not walk without support was assisted by an asthmatic and by a boy with a deformed arm. It was a great day for everyone, just to be there and look, and this was a fitting culmination to the week.

The course was an overwhelming success and the main lesson learned was plain: as long as there were no medical reasons to the contrary, experienced instructors could introduce a great many physically handicapped people to a large range of outdoor pursuits. The presence of a handicap meant that for each individual the circumstances in which he or she took part had to be carefully chosen. Experienced, able-bodied canoeists might go down a fast, cold river while a handicapped person might never progress beyond paddling around a still lake in summer. As a hard climber scales a big north face, a spastic girl may be scrambling over easy rock, with a rope, or hill-walking. The important common factor is that each person can find enjoyment and fulfilment within their limitations. I believe that anyone with a physical handicap needs to avoid injury more carefully than an able-bodied counterpart, because an additional handicap, even temporary, may affect him or her more. But, on the other hand, there is a danger that over-protection may condemn that person to a life which they feel is hardly worth living. Somewhere between these extremes a balance must be struck, and the balance must depend a great deal on the choice of the adult individual.

That course at Plas y Brenin symbolised all I had hoped for; the participants had a taste of what I had had for many years from climbing. No special organisation had been set up, for this was a system by which disabled people could be integrated in ordinary centres. In fact, plans were made for some people to go back to the centre. As a course adviser, I was content.

I tried four new activities which I hoped to continue: canoeing, sailing, ski-bobbing and cross-country skiing. The last sport, on the seven hundred metre artificial track at the centre, was a straightforward process of sliding the skis and pushing with the poles. It would make a handy way of crossing glaciers in a third of the time I take on soft snow, and I began to weigh up the advantages and disadvantages of skis and snow-shoes.

Thinking about covering long distances raised a question: How far could I walk in a day? On the John o' Groats to Land's End walk the maximum was sixteen miles. Had several years of climbing and walking pushed up my range? There was only one way to find out and so, one Sunday morning, Judy and I began to lap Regent's Park. Each circuit was two point seven miles. Track-suited runners padded past on the same footpath, giraffes' heads swayed above the fences at the zoo, huge coloured birds screamed and chattered, and squirrels scampered through the trees. It was dawn at the start and dusk at the finish, and we did more than eight laps, twenty-two and a half miles in all, and could have gone on for longer.

At the limb centre my artificial legs, which had had a very hard life for thirteen years, were condemned and I received two new pairs. I kept one of the old pairs for some tests on the effects of falling in water. The results were definite: even with a water-wing blown up inside each leg, I sank.

"You've got three pairs of legs now," someone remarked. "That makes you a wingless insect."

The old legs had been made rather short, leaving a disproportionate shortness from the knees down. Being one and a half inches longer, the new legs made walking seem easier because the swing of the limbs felt more natural than with shorter legs. I strutted about on the new legs and waited for friends to notice the new, taller Norm. Three successive people stared and said, "Have you changed your hair style?"

Naturally, I wanted to see what difference the increased height would make to climbing, so at Christmas 1973 Judy and I went to Cornwall to climb on the cliffs at Cligga, near

Perranporth. I had lived within a mile of that particular bit of coast for several years but although I had seen it from a glider I had never visited the area.

Many years before one of my grandfathers had found parts of a body in a cove at Cligga. He was unemployed at the time and had gone there to collect driftwood when he came across pieces of human limbs. Detectives were summoned from Scotland Yard, the remains were identified as those of a woman, and enquiries went on for a long time. It was never established how the pieces came to be there; one theory was that the woman had fallen from a ship and been cut to pieces by the propeller.

A climb called Discretion attracted me. I was able to fix up a good belay at the top of the cliff so Judy could hold the rope from above. She was very experienced in that role, even though she was not keen on climbing herself. Descending by an easy way, I had a look at the route. The lower rock was a bit damp but higher up was dry. I shouted to Judy that I was ready to start.

The climb began on a slippery slab composed of firm, black rock leading sharply up for a dozen feet or more. Big holds allowed

244

strenuous heaves with the arms. It was a simple start, but I knew it would get harder because the route was graded Severe. I soon found out why.

Judy sat in the sun at the top. It was Christmas Eve, and very cold where the sunshine did not fall. As I rose, she took in the slack rope.

Where the slab narrowed at the top it was necessary to step to the right, around a corner. The rock was poor, very brittle, but noticeably so. There was no deception: the rock looked unreliable and was, and if it were not for the state of the granite the climb would have been given a lower grade. Provided I was careful the risk was not great. I had often come across worse rock in the Alps but routes in Britain usually keep to firmer terrain.

I clung to friable holds while standing on dubious steps on a steep face. Like old, tired concrete the rock crumbled and fell away in tiny pieces. The route was only sixty feet and in a few minutes I was ten feet below Judy. She looked down and said, "Well done. That's the third Severe you've done."

"I haven't finished yet."

The rock did not improve and there was

hardly a hold that could be relied on completely. Right up to the very last move to the safety of a grass ledge care was required. It was with a feeling of relief that I finally sat on the ledge.

"Well, I didn't notice any difference with these new legs, but obviously they give me a better reach," I told Judy.

As a result of a conversation about climbing, a friend, Lou, manufactured some metal plates to fit in the bottoms of my climbing boots. This meant that I could wear boots with flexible soles for walking, then put plates in the boots to stiffen them for climbing. Thus was solved a big problem as I had found walking to be difficult in stiff-soled boots and climbing to be very difficult in boots with flexible soles. With the addition of some strong miner's knee pads scrounged from my father-in-law, I was ready to climb. I guessed that the plates would be useful but I had to put them to the test before I could be sure.

Off to Bosigran, Cornwall, for the club's usual Easter trip. Dave and I did Oread, 175 feet, and the metal plates made a great difference. The first pitch was quite short. I joined Dave on the ledge thirty feet up the cliff.

"Those plates helped a lot," he said. "You're climbing three times as fast."

"It's easier. Less exhausting. Let's see how the plates are standing up to the wear."

Removing my right boot, I took the plate out and held it up. The plate was not bent at all. As I leaned to put the boot on again I dropped it and the plate.

"Below!" we bellowed, as the boot and plate tumbled down. There were some climbers at the bottom of the cliff. Fortunately the boot and plate missed them by several feet.

"Excuse me," I called down. "If you're coming up this way would you mind bringing up my boot? And the foot-shaped piece of metal near it."

One of them returned my possessions as he came up the route, and he was very good natured about nearly being hit by them.

The wall above, climbed on small holds, was no problem and apart from one move on which I dithered for a while, it was by far the easiest time I had ever had on that grade of climb, Very Difficult.

Also at Bosigran we did Ledge Climb, 170

feet, Very Difficult. Up a crack in the granite for close on thirty feet, then rising leftward up the cliff on abundant holds to belay beneath the overhang. Dave squeezed into the chimney above me.

"My gut won't fit," he called down, but he was up quickly. Another pitch to thirty feet above that, and we were on the clifftop. No problems; knee pads and plates were just the job, and Lou made some more in a very lightweight material. The Severe bug bit, and Dave and I went to an outcrop at Penallta in South Wales.

"We'll try Devils in Hell," he said. "It's Hard Severe, but I think it's a bit overgraded." Hard Severe is at the top end of the Severe grade.

He led quickly. The climb went up a steep wall to start, following a crack, and over a bulge which was not hard because of one huge and conveniently placed handhold.

"The awkward bit is just below me," Dave shouted from the belay forty-five feet up.

It was awkward, but easier with knee pads than it might have been to get up the holdless bulge. I reached Dave.

The route finished up an easy corner, but Dave decided to take a harder way, traversing left and then up an arête. I took quite a long time on one move where I had to reach a high hold with both hands and swing around a corner but to cries of "Come on, you bugger!" from above it was soon finished.

"Well that's the recipe," I said. "The right boots, metal plates and knee pads give a chance of doing a few Severes. That's the fourth one."

Yet there was an important ingredient missing from that recipe. Despite finding the right bits of equipment to help on harder routes I was concerned about one weakness, a weakness which lay within me. I had failed some Severe routes and failure would come again unless I could commit myself more. A couple of times, like a discontented hen trying to find a way over a stone hedge and into a cornfield, I had scratched about and wandered back and forth, getting only a little way up some Severe routes, searching for others and attacking them fruitlessly, then slinking away disappointed. Understandably, even a short fall on metal legs was likely to have serious consequences, but by climbing second this danger could be reduced. Still, I had to remember that in many circumstances, even with the protection of the rope, a fall could do a lot of damage. Careful choice of routes and steady climbing could lower the risk to a level I was prepared to accept, but it was my attitude, more than physical limitations, holding me back on Severe climbs. I had to strike the delicate balance at the point at which I was climbing at my utmost limit without overstepping the mark. It was with these thoughts uppermost in my mind that I persuaded Judy to volunteer to hold the rope at Brean Down, in Somerset. The down is a pleasant little peninsula, one and a half miles long and a quarter of a mile wide. Wild thyme, scabious, fern and bramble provide food and cover for many creatures there, including rabbits, field mice, shrews, voles, common blue butterflies, skylarks, kestrels. In some places there are steep cliffs, in others the peninsula meets the sea gently. We found the Red Slab, stretching steeply down into the sea. The reason for the name of that particular stretch of cliff was obvious, although in the brilliant sunlight it looked more pink than red. It was low, no more than thirty feet, and the limestone sloped at about seventy degrees. Meeting the slab on the right edge and at right angles to it was a vertical wall, so the slab and wall formed a steep corner. In that corner, from top to bottom, was a crack large enough to get a hand in, and that was where the route went. Red Slab Corner was graded at the easy end of the Severe standard.

The sea splashed over the bottom of the slab. Judy was safely belayed at the top, and I descended by an easy route to the start.

"When you're ready, Norm."

"Climbing."

Facing right, with fingers in the crack, I leaned back to take much of the weight on my arms. The soles of my boots began to walk up the vertical wall. When climbing in this way, or laybacking, the feet are placed high, close to the hands. Feet and hands are raised alternately. It was a strenuous way to gain height and soon I was pleased to find a good ledge for a handhold on the wall. By jamming my hands in the crack I was able to pull up and get the right foot on that ledge, and with a knee pad pressed on the slab I was in a safe position. I jammed my hands higher in the crack and pulled up again. The toe of the right boot just fitted the crack, but I was suddenly in trouble: the left knee pad slipped down and hung around my ankle. It was not possible to reach down and strap it on again because I could not spare a hand for the job at the time, particularly as I had only one foothold.

I was perhaps ten feet up the slab and here was a reason to decide that retreat was appropriate. Without the pad a knee pressed on the rock would most likely have slipped.

It was time to believe that I could go on, time to really convince myself that Severe routes were within my limits. No matter how hard I thought I had tried in the past I would have to try harder. There was a great difference between, "I'll try to climb this", and "I'm going to climb this".

Tiny toeholds on the vertical wall and on the slab raised me a few more feet, and with the right foot on a good ledge, as big in area as a playing card, and the right hand in a pocket hold like a letterbox, there was an opportunity to rest.

"The left pad's off."

"Oh, what a shame. You all right?"

"Yes. So far. I'll rest for a while and work out what to do next."

Although I could rest I was not able to release either of the precious hand holds to reach down and fix the pad. It was clear that this was just the situation in which the left pad would be helpful. There were few footholds on that side and the pad would have given plenty of friction on the slab.

The security of the little ledge and the pocket hold had to be left behind. For two minutes, three, four, I worked out what moves I would make. Above my left knee was a small hold. If you stuck a pencil in a horizontal position on the rock it would have provided a similar area and shape to stand on. In the crack a triangular bit of rock, the size of a large thumbnail, stuck out and begged to be stepped on. Without the plates in my boots there would have been little chance of using those holds.

With both hands jammed in the crack I pulled up, losing a bit of skin from my knuckles but gaining a few inches of height. It was a huge step up at the same time for the left leg. Muscles were stretched as tight as bowstrings and extreme effort made me cry out like someone in agony. The left boot made contact and held on the pencil sized hold.

"You all right, Norm?"

"Yes."

She was only eight or nine feet above. The right boot settled on the thumbnail.

What a stupid sport! And I loved every moment of it.

Another minute crept by as I rested. All the way up energetic bursts had been punctuated by pauses while strength returned.

The rock became more friendly, yielding holds where I wanted them: a big pocket hold on the wall, then another, and footholds on the slab. In a few easy moves I was up. Thank God!

A mere thirty feet, but shortness did not make it any easier technically. Short routes can be very hard.

"Seems a bit daft really. Over twenty minutes to get up that piddling little thing. But now I know I can do more Severes, even though I can't lead them."

Suddenly a question formed in my mind. Why can't I lead them? Go away, silly question. But it came back. Why can't I lead them? Well, there was the danger of a fall, and the consequences could be very serious because I could not land well. I had never had an unexpected fall of more than two or three feet. On very steep or overhanging rock I had often attempted routes on which I had known that I was likely to slip at some point, and had set up the rope in such a way that I fell clear of the rock and dangled, rather than landing on a ledge or the ground on my legs. I had fallen, for instance, out of an overhanging crack and parted company with an awkward bulge in a vertical chimney, and had dropped to safety on to the rope. To lead, there were two important considerations: could I find routes on which I could protect myself against falling on my legs, and was I prepared to take the extra risk? I realised that the answer to both questions was yes. If I did not keep hammering away at what I found hard then I would not improve.

The most common form of protection against a fall used nowadays is the metal chockstone or nut, which is threaded on a wire or rope loop to form a "runner". Their use is simple: climb up a few feet, reach a small crack, wedge a nut in the crack and pass the main climbing rope through a karabiner clipped to the loop. When this has been done the man below can hold you on what amounts to a simple pulley system, if the nut stays in place. When you climb several feet above the nut and then fall, you will drop well below the nut before the rope can be pulled tight from beneath. Stories of falling runners abound and one of the most interesting I have heard concerned one of the climbers from the South Wales Mountaineering Club, Mike. He was eighty feet up a wall at the Taff's Well Quarry, standing on a loop of nylon tape clipped to a piton when the piton fell out and he fell down. The anchors for his runners: another piton, a sapling and a thick ivy stalk. Each gave way in succession, and would not have held him for long because he had dislodged a large block which narrowly missed the second man and cut the rope in two. Mike dropped forty-five feet, past the second man, and was heading for serious injury or death on the ground thirty-five feet below. Still around Mike's ankle was the loop he had been standing on, and just by the second man's feet was a small tree stump. The loop caught over that stump and Mike's fall was arrested. He dangled head down, unhurt.

To Churchill Rocks I went again, this time with Tim Burton, a roughneck on a North Sea oil rig. He was in his mid-twenties and had not had much climbing experience.

"Good. The rock's dry. I'll lead the Diagonal Route, from the bottom left corner of the slab to the top right corner. A hundred and twenty feet. Mild Severe," I told Tim. "It doesn't look like the best route for protection but on a slab like this I'll slide and tumble about if I slip. That's better than dropping straight down and hitting the deck."

The type of climbing was familiar, on tiny holds or no holds at all except for the friction of hands, toes and knee pads on sloping rock. As soon as possible, perhaps fifteen feet up, a nut was coaxed into a tiny crack. There was no certainty that it would stay in place if I fell but I was confident that I would not, provided it remained dry. The cloudy sky did not threaten rain within the next half-hour. I got thirty feet up and the nut gave no protection; a slip, and I would hit the ground before the rope went tight. Unfortunately as I went higher there was no place for another nut. Forty feet, fifty feet, sixty feet and still no runner, but I judged that I would not slip. A minute or two more and in went another nut; again it was not possible to place it in such a way as to be absolutely secure. The movement of the rope had caused the lower runner to drop out. However, there was comfort soon: two-thirds of the way up the slab, or perhaps a little less, was a crack which took a large nut.

"Got a good runner on, Tim."

The crack gave a couple of nice holds, then I kept going, up and to the right. The climbing became easier and before long I was taking in the rope as Tim followed quickly up. It had not been as hard as I had anticipated. Now I was truly through the mental barrier which had held me back. Good able-bodied climbers might sneer at someone who was pushed to lead Mild Severe, yet I was toying with my upper limits.

Tim went down and up by a different route, down again and up, while I belayed.

"I'd like to lead the Right Hand Route now, Tim."

It felt so easy: thirty feet without being able to place a runner, but I was still confident. And suddenly, down came heavy rain to make the rock very slippery.

"Hell! Better get down from here!"

With each movement in descent I thought, that foot may hold, or it may not. Tim was twelve feet below when away went my feet, flopping me face down on the rock. Like a human toboggan I shot feet first towards the ground. Whoosh! All the way down I wondered what would happen at the moment when rigid legs struck the ground. Tim slowed me a bit as I reached the bottom of the slab and I crashed into the earth. For a few seconds I lay there waiting to feel pain, but none came. I was unhurt.

In the same day I had led a climb for the first time and had had a short fall to remind me of my vulnerability. It seemed appropriate.

With the move to leading a whole new area of rock climbing opened up. In Cornwall, with John Hodgkins from the South Wales club, I led the first sixty feet pitch of Alison Rib, a Diff. at Bosigran. Large, comforting knobs and holes, and many places for runners all the way up, gave good protection against a fall. At the top of that pitch it started to rain, so John took over and led us quickly a hundred feet to the top. Next with Judy at Swanage, Dorset, on an area of cliff called Cattle Troughs, I tried another Diff. route known as Chimney. As its name suggests it was a chimney, and tight near the top. Where the chimney ended there was easy rock. Judy was not in a mood to follow so I descended the way I had come and removed the nut runners. All that day I led little bits, never going more than twenty or thirty feet up, and the following day at Winspit cove in Dorset was taken up with similar leading practice on short problems. Unlike the climber with legs, it was wise for me to use as much protection as possible on the first few feet to avoid hitting the rock below if I fell. It was no use thinking I could drop five or six feet on to rock and get away unharmed. At the end of the day my sore, swollen, pink fingers looked like two bunches of sausages, and muscles ached all over my body. The day was well spent; I had led a few routes and would lead more.

9

SUMMER approached and I put my thoughts to the coming alpine season. On arriving home from work one day Judy found me walking about with a bath tray strapped to each foot.

"What on earth are you doing?"

"Snow-shoes. Lighter than the ones you can buy. But I think plastic may be a bit slippery on snow."

"You look pretty silly like that."

In any case it took just a few minutes of walking to split the bath trays, and in the long run it turned out better to buy a ready-made pair.

The Matterhorn had been on my mind all year. After climbing to the Solvay hut I had asked at the Zermatt guides' office if a guide could be found for the following year and the man there said it would be all right. However, when I wrote to the office to confirm this I received no reply.

The London editor of a Swiss news agency contacted me to see what I had planned for the summer.

261

"The Matterhorn. But I don't know if any guides will go, and even if they do I can't afford to pay them. And none of my friends are going to Zermatt this year."

Because of a way of life which left enough time to do two things I very much wanted to do, climb and write the outdoor pursuits guide, my annual earnings were only £500.

A couple of years before I had written half a dozen letters to large business organisations to request funds for a climbing trip. I was always rather uncertain about writing these letters because I couldn't really believe that anyone would be prepared to take the responsibility of being associated with one of my climbs, and I couldn't see why someone else should pay for my excitement and pleasure. The response from the firms was three dozen cans of beer and the offer of a free tin of antiseptic ointment.

The Swiss editor of the agency was sufficiently interested in the proposed climb to be prepared to pay the guide fees. Unfortunately the President of the Zermatt guides then decided that the ascent was too dangerous for me. True, like anyone else attempting the Matterhorn I could be killed or injured, but it was unlikely.

Eventually contact was made with Hans Kaufmann, with whom I had climbed the Eiger; he would go.

Brian Campbell gave my legs the usual, thorough, pre-alpine check at the limb centre, and less than twenty-four hours after leaving Victoria Station I was nearly ten thousand feet above sea level at the Gandegg hut, reached easily in twenty minutes' walk from a cable car out of Zermatt. August was not quite halfway through.

Training at altitude was essential and the next day I sat on the moraine at the edge of the Theodul glacier and waited to hitch a lift across with anyone who would let me join their rope. The glacier is not especially dangerous to cross but on rare occasions people do fall in crevasses there. No more than five minutes went by and two Germans and their wives came along. They knew what I was waiting for.

"You vant to go to zee Theodul hut?"

"Yes please."

"You can come vis us."

We rose slowly through a thousand feet in a gradual pull up the snow and crevassed ice. Skiers hissed downhill making us look out of place, like snails caught in the snow. In one and a half hours we crossed the high frontier as the mountaineer smugglers used to, into Italy.

There was no opportunity to get to know my companions, who took a look around the hut, and said something like, "Filthy Italians!" and marched back down the glacier. For a mountain hut the place seemed acceptable and another group of German people soon included me in their company.

"You are going up the Breithorn to-morrow?"

The question came from Gunter, a serious yet cheerful man of forty who worked as a judge. The Breithorn, 13,660 feet (4,165 metres), was close and the normal route was easy but all on snow.

"No. I am alone."

"Come with us then," Hans said. He was a priest.

"I am slow, particularly on a snow route."

Although I explained why and they appeared to have understood, it turned out that they had not.

"You can come with us," Hans reaffirmed.

So at half past five the next day I roped up with Gunter and his friend, Franz. On another rope were Hans, two young ladies and Bernhard, an apprentice railway worker.

There must have been forty or more people trudging the same way. For my sake, I believed, Gunter set a very slow pace—too slow for me because I found it impossible to get into a good rhythm.

A short, steep, icy slope, a gentle gradient, a stretch of moderately steep snow, a couple of crevasses to step over, a plateau of softening snow: an easy route, yet for me quite hard. Much of the way was just a walk over gentle white undulations, and there was always a good view of the surrounding peaks if we lifted our eyes. Hours went quickly.

"You can go faster if you like," I explained to Gunter, but we kept the same pace, and by the time we had pulled ourselves up the final steepish snow to the summit five hours had gone by. It was certainly one of the easiest to reach of alpine summits over the four thousand metre mark. Franz produced a tin of delicious raspberries for us to share on the top, and later we had a tin of pineapple chunks which Bernhard had brought.

On the descent Gunter stayed with me while the others hurried to catch the cable car to the valley. The climb was a useful training exercise and was valuable in one more important respect: as we headed back to the hut I tried out the snow-shoes. They were ideal, and would see a lot of snow over the next few years. If I had taken them to Mont Blanc or on the glaciers beneath the Jungfrau and the Wellenkuppe those ascents and descents would have been transformed into the easiest of climbs.

"Is one of your legs hurt?" Gunter enquired.

I explained again.

"Now I understand," he said. Obviously they had all misunderstood what I had told them the night before. "And still you love to go to the mountains."

"Oh yes. As much as anyone. More than most, I believe."

"I understand."

On the dawdle back across the plateau Gunter called a halt a couple of times so we could just sit and look. I had never met such a man for taking his time and stopping to savour every moment. Even when a fifteen minute hailstorm thrashed at us he plodded on in his unhurrying pace. In fact we took so long that we were out for ten hours that day.

Back in Zermatt I booked in at a dormitory at the top of the Bahnhof Hotel, and rang

Herr Perll, the Swiss editor of the news agency. He was a mountaineer and intended taking pictures on the climb. He was away for three days, I learned.

I mooched around Zermatt. The weather stayed fine and the climbing boomed. For three or four days the Matterhorn was thronged with mountaineers, and then the weather turned nasty. I had missed my chance. Damn, damn, damn.

On ringing Herr Perll again I was told he was still away on holiday, so I moved to a dormitory in a mountain hotel at Gornergrat and spent three days walking about at around the ten thousand feet contour.

Down to Zermatt again. On the telephone to Herr Perll.

"I will come to Zermatt on Wednesday," he said.

Three more days to wait, to wander about. In the basement of the hotel was a kitchen where you could cook for yourself, and it was there that one day a very distinguished visitor appeared: Lord Hunt. In company with his wife and a friend he was planning to travel over to Chamonix across the mountains. As a result of our meeting there Lord Hunt later came to the press launch of the outdoor pursuits guide. Sir Roger Bannister, at that time Chairman of the Sports Council, was at the launch too, so with the leader of the successful British Everest expedition and the first man to run a mile in four minutes at the same event we were not short of famous personalities. And it was very appropriate that the foreword to the guide was written by Sir Jack Longland, who used to climb with one-legged Geoffrey Winthrop Young.

It was tempting to go and do some more high peaks, but I had to stay around to be ready to climb the Matterhorn. I could not risk doing too much in training for fear of damage to the stumps. Instead of going up the high peaks I made do with easy ascents in the area: twice I went up the Ober Rothorn, 11,250 feet (3,415 metres), and twice up the Unter Rothorn, 10,200 feet (3,103 metres). Mostly I went alone because these were safe, busy trails, and once with Jon Ryder, an exceptionally fit American who became so fond of Zermatt that he stayed on to work on the Gornergrat railway for the winter.

Days crept by. In the brief spells when the weather was fine Hans Kaufmann considered that conditions on the Matterhorn were not good enough for me. The weather was never stable for long, and then there was another setback: Hans Kaufmann said he was busy for several days so could not go even if the weather was suitable. The Zermatt guide who would have gone with him was busy too. Whether they were really busy or had had second thoughts I could not say, but I had to start looking for guides again. I'm not superstitious but the day on which this news came was Friday, September 13th.

I had been in Switzerland five weeks and was still waiting. I was always bloody well waiting, it seemed.

A few 'phone calls led me to get in touch with Eddy Petrig, a guide. He had heard that I was in the village so there was no need for long explanations.

"When do you want to go?" he asked.

"As soon as possible."

"We will meet tomorrow and talk. I cannot say yet that I will go."

We met the next day and sat on a low wall outside the Bahnhof Hotel to talk about the climbing I had done.

"How long do you think you will need to get to the summit?"

"Seven and a half or eight hours. Perhaps more." Geoffrey Winthrop Young took nine and a half hours to the summit, eighteen hours for the return trip in conditions better than had been seen for many years. Was my estimate too optimistic? And one guide who knew Geoffrey told me that the ascent had been very difficult for him and caused many problems for his guides.

"I would like to go," Eddy said at last. "I will contact another guide to be with us."

"That's fine."

"And I will ring you when it is time to go."

Eddy was influenced, I believe, by the fact that he felt that the guides had not behaved properly in not replying to my letter.

Frau Biner, who usually ran the Bahnhof Hotel, was convalescing after breaking a thigh, so two of her relations, Kathy and Miriam, looked after the place. Being amongst the longest staying guests that year, Jon and I were treated with special kindness, and the friendliness of many people is one of the things I remember most about the trip to Zermatt.

"If you climb the Matterhorn you will be very happy," Miriam said one day. "And if you cannot it will make me very sad."

The weather forecast gave no cause for optimism for a couple of days. September

17th arrived and my sixth week in Switzerland began.

"What's the matter with you?" Eddy's wife asked him with irritation. "You're out looking at the weather every fifteen minutes!"

He admitted to me later that he had been very anxious while waiting. I was under a strain too.

"I feel like my stomach's connected to the barometer," I told Jon. "Every time I see it go up or down my guts do too."

"You'll do it if the weather gives you a chance," Jon insisted.

Still the weather would not let me go, and waiting was getting me down. A feeling of utter desolation gripped me. Anyone who has set his heart on a dear goal and has been frustrated day after day, week after week, will understand what I mean. I lay on my bunk and tried to convince myself that to climb the Matterhorn was insignificant, but, selfishly, the one thing I really wanted in life at the time was to stand on the top of the Matterhorn.

"Hallo! Telephone!"

It was the Spanish houskeeper, a large, friendly lady, calling me.

Eddy was on the line.

"The weather is not really settled but we should go," he said. "You should ring Herr Perll and get him to come to to Zermatt now. Otherwise you may not get a chance this year."

Götz Perll arrived the same day. Bearded, dark, of average build, thirty-four years old. Gradually scraps of information built up a picture of the man: independent, determined, married five years with one baby of nine months, originally from Germany, fond of skiing.

The next day was September 20th. At eight a.m. thick mist cut off the sky. By half past nine the same morning it was raining lightly. Eddy rang at ten a.m.

"We will wait until the forecast at half past twelve. There has been some snow at the Hörnli hut."

"If not this year, then next year," I said. Like the grains of sand in an egg-timer, minutes were running out. If they ran out completely it would be next year before the timer could be turned over to start again.

Eddy was definite: "I want you to do it this year now you are trained."

The barometer fell a little. Oh dear! And by noon it was raining again. At one o'clock the 'phone rang and Götz picked it up. He talked seriously for a minute or two, and as he talked he raised one thumb in the air.

"We go to the Belvedere Hotel this afternoon," he said. "Eddy is very confident that you can do it but it depends on the weather."

In haste we bought food for the trip, had a good meal and hurried off to the cable car, where Eddy waited with Richard Biner, an aspirant guide who was to climb with Götz. Richard did not speak much English and was a quiet man.

Eddy stared at my boots. They were light, ideal for me but too light for a mountaineer with real feet.

"Don't your feet get cold with those boots?"

"I suppose so. But it doesn't matter."

"Of course. I am stupid."

He was an amazingly young-looking man. At first I thought he was in his mid-forties but in fact he was fifty-seven years old. He was not the type who bulged with muscle; this lean, agile person moved in a deliberate, cat-like way and it was difficult to believe that in most societies he would be only a few years from retirement. Eddy had travelled to several countries and had lived some years in

Canada. He had been married a few years, and perhaps his young children helped him to remain as young in mind as he looked in body. He seemed to belong more to my generation than to his own.

A cable car whisked us up through light rain, up 3,000 feet in minutes to Schwarzee, at about 8,500 feet (2,582 metres). A thick mist blanket hung greyly over the area.

"It is no good. We must go down," Eddy said, but he was not serious and led the way up the trail.

"You can go in front and make the pace if you like, Norman. Go as slowly as you like," he suggested, and within five minutes said, "Don't go so fast. I don't want you pooped for tomorrow."

"Going too slowly makes it more difficult. It's like doing press-ups: the slow ones are harder."

"All right. You know what is best for you."

Down in Zermatt a chimney sweep called at the Bahnhof Hotel.

"That is good luck," Miriam told Jon. "Now I know Norman will succeed. The chimney sweep is always a sign of good luck.

For an hour we tramped on in single file. The mist thinned. It was wonderfully cool for walking. Snow and ice lay on the zigzags of the Hörnli buttress.

"The wind is from the north," Eddy announced. "The weather will be good tomorrow. That is because you are an angel without wings. You are lucky. And you did not say you could do more than you can when I talked to you. Now I am excited. As long as the weather is all right you will do it."

The weather. Always the weather. If one heavy snow shower came the route would probably not be in condition again that year.

We were at the Belvedere Hotel in one and a half hours. The manager and his wife had kindly promised to keep the hotel open for an extra night the following day, the day on which, if all went well, we should either get back or be staying in the Solvay hut. This brought home to me just how close we were to the end of the season.

A man arrived at the hotel.

"Norman, this is Leo Imesch," Eddy said. "He will be going with us."

Leo was broad, tall, fair, about twenty-five years old, a kind and cheerful man with a big moustache. He hoped to qualify as a guide the next year.

So there we were: the incredibly young

Eddy, Götz, who had made the event possible, the cheerful and enthusiastic Leo, quiet Richard, and me. Fools or realists? The next day would show.

The hotel manager kept offering me wine but I drank tea instead. His wife prepared a very substantial meal. Suitably fed, we went to look at the weather again. Stars stood out sharply over mist-filled valleys.

"It will be good," Eddy said once more.

I turned in early, and while I slept Eddy and the hotel manager argued about my chances. Eddy was confident, the manager was not, but still gave Leo a bottle of strong spirit for us to share in celebration if we reached the summit. We would learn the irony of that argument the next day.

The sound of someone laughing quietly awoke me in the morning; my legs, still wearing trousers, leaned against the bottom of my bunk as if resting too, and caused much amusement.

Yesterday's trail walk had lifted us through more than two thousand feet. Now the real climbing would begin, four thousand feet up the jagged Hörnli ridge, keeping mostly to the left side, at other times moving on the crest of the ridge. This was roughly the route of the first ascent more than a hundred years before, when four of the party of seven fell to their deaths on the way down.

Five a.m. Not light, but not black. Eddy led, with me and then Leo behind. Richard led Götz. The weather refused to let us know for sure that it would remain good, but the signs were reasonably favourable.

Three people left the hotel in front of us: the manager and two friends.

Thick snow had accumulated on the normal way near the hotel. Throughout the usual climbing season the rock there would have been clear but now we crunched over a firm, white covering.

Ice made the first steep rock more difficult, and obviously the whole route would be more icy than usual. It had been considerably easier when I was with Dave.

"Numerous short pitches of II" the guidebook said. II is equivalent to Moderate, and we started up the first of those pitches. I saw little of the surroundings apart from the rock, ice and snow under my boots and hands, and I remember the mountain only in bits and pieces. There was a vertical pitch, short and not hard, there was a bit of track through broken rock, there were stretches of snow-covered, sloping rock and more steep rock with good holds.

Eddy had climbed one ridge of the Matterhorn, the Zmutt, fifty-two times, and had often used the Hörnli ridge for descent. With one companion he made the first winter ascent of the Zmutt ridge in 1948.

Head torches were soon extinguished. Unlike on my previous trek that way there had been no long line of lights ahead of us, and the absence of other climbers meant there was little need to wear helmets as a protection against stonefall.

I had to push myself to keep up a reasonable pace. After half an hour, an hour, an hour and a half, two hours, it would have been too easy to drop back to a more comfortable pace, but it was essential to press on so we would be as high as possible as quickly as was sensible.

"Go as you like," Eddy emphasised. "You know what you are able to do," and soon after he said, "I think you should go a little more slowly. It is a long way."

"All right. I'll treat it like steady, gentle sex. But don't be surprised if I rush a bit towards the end."

He laughed and said, "While you talk

like that I know everything is all right."

"You are doing well," Leo added in encouragement.

Götz did not request any hesitation for photographs, but took them as we went. We climbed and scrambled without interruption and that made it easier to keep going. Sometimes Götz and Richard were ahead and sometimes they were behind.

Another pitch of Moderate rock, and another, until we were directly below the Salvay hut. The three men who had been ahead of us turned back because the hotel manager was feeling unwell.

Ahead was the Moseley Slab, at the top of which, the route description said, was a near-vertical corner to climb. Here, or on the slab above, one of Geoffry Winthrop Young's guides had fallen and was saved on the rope by another guide. On an earlier occasion a guide accompanying one of Geoffrey's friends, Sir Arnold Lunn, fell at the same spot. Sir Arnold and the guide were saved by another guide on the same rope. The slab was named after an American doctor who was killed there. All went well for us and we were soon seated inside the wooden Solvay hut, 13,120 feet (4,000 metres) high. Three and a half hours from the bottom of the ridge. Not bad.

We sipped hot tea from flasks and ate little bits: cheese, dried fruit, meat.

Götz asked, "How do you feel?"

"Fine. This sort of route really suits me."

"Do you think we'll make it?" I asked Leo.

"If the weather is all right."

There was mist higher up. For the time being, at least, the weather was satisfactory.

How lucky we were that there were no other climbers around: no stonefall, and we had the peak to ourselves without delays on the harder sections. It felt right. My major disappointment with the route, that it was crowded, did not apply that day.

In a few minutes we were on our way again, up the Upper Moseley Slab, fifty feet, steep and graded Moderate. Then there was one of the few exposed, narrow rock ridges to walk and scramble over. More scrambling and easy climbing brought us in half an hour to the Shoulder, a large snow and ice slope at forty-five degrees. Time for crampons. At intervals of a hundred feet or more large metal stanchions had been driven in as belay anchors. Eddy went ahead from stanchion to stanchion and I followed only when he had the rope around one of them.

Down in Zermatt, nine thousand feet below, Miriam was watching through a telescope. She picked us out against the white backcloth of the Shoulder, and was even able to see that the second man on the first rope was hunched over moving quite slowly. She knew who that was.

On the Shoulder a familiar feeling of nausea began to bother me. I think this was caused by physical effort because six hours of any exertion which really makes you puff is quite a strain. So there was the nausea barrier to be faced again. In one way it would have been easy to have stopped but ambition drove me on. At the same time it was as if the decision had been taken away from me; the Matterhorn would not let me rest. It was silly to believe that the mountain was in charge, because the ambition was within me, but it felt as if the Matterhorn would not release me until I reached the top.

Cold, firm snow held reassuringly at each step. It took several minutes to get up the Shoulder. More climbing on rock brought us abruptly to the edge of the north face, plunging down on our right, but we hardly hesitated to look.

Leo and Eddy were talking to each other cheerfully in German; obviously they were optimistic. Now I was confident too.

Next to overcome was a section with fixed ropes. I knew that afterwards there was only a steep rock and snow slope to the summit.

Pulling up on the fixed rope was very tiring, many people had told me, and certainly I found it to be hard work. The ropes hung permanently down the steep rock and were ice-coated in places. Without crampons it would have been difficult to have kept our feet firmly on the icy rock as we hauled ourselves up hand over hand. I felt that the route would have been more enjoyable without those ropes, although in icy conditions I was pleased to use them. Without the ropes it would have been for me a very serious expedition.

"My mother worries when I am here," Leo remarked. "My uncle was killed on the Matterhorn when a fixed rope broke. On the Italian side."

Up a rope, heave, heave, heave, with gloved hands, up another and another. There was a last vertical pitch to pull up at the top

282

of that section, and then we were on the slope known as the Roof.

Only the Roof to go. I would make it! I would make it!

From then on it was a scramble over rock and snow. Loose rock and snow moved under our feet.

"It's not far now," Leo said, pointing upwards. "That's the summit."

Four or five minutes to the top, it appeared.

"Can't go on!" I joked.

We were moving quickly. My ambition was almost at rest, but not quite. Another glance up at the top, a rapid, triumphant scramble and there we were, on the summit of the Matterhorn, 14,690 feet (4,477 metres). The sharp summit was almost horizontal and approached a hundred yards in length, with flanks falling away steeply for thousands of feet on either side. Seven and a quarter hours from the hotel was slightly less than I had expected in those conditions.

Everyone was grinning.

"I know this sounds silly but I don't know whether to laugh or cry," I said.

"You do what you like. We understand. It is a very happy day for us too," Eddy told me, and Leo added, "This is one of the best days I have ever had on the mountains."

Götz looked thrilled and declared that this was one of the happiest days of his life. It was his first time on the Matterhorn.

I laughed quietly, frequently, like someone with a secret. I was released and had no need to return next year.

As we shook hands all round Götz clicked away with his camera. Moving a few feet below the summit to escape the bitter wind we sat on rock to nibble at food and drink tea. The bottle of spirit supplied by the hotel manager was forgotten.

No one else reached the summit that day. We had met three men who turned back and later saw two more who got to the Shoulder before going down again.

Cloud blocked our view of Zermatt but we could see Mont Blanc. A red helicopter chattered by, quite close, and people inside waved. We waved back and I thought how pleasant it would have been to tell them how contented we were; but we were isolated. The aircraft flew down and was soon out of sight behind cloud. Before long we followed the same general direction, downwards.

"Can we get back to the hotel today and

miss the Solvay hut?" Eddy wanted to know.

"I think so."

Our elation was understandable but we had done only half of the job. Now we had to get down safely. We descended the Roof and the fixed ropes with reasonable speed. On narrow ridges we tried a new method: Leo would walk while I lightly rested a hand on his rucksack to help balance. In this way we moved quite rapidly on airy ridges.

We passed two climbers who had reached the Shoulder. I took shameful but human pleasure from the fact that we were the only successful party on the mountain that day. Difficulties in route finding had slowed this pair, and they failed to get back to the hotel that night.

Eddy and Leo remained patient, vigilant, good-humoured. The Solvay hut was reached in what for me was a sprint time, two hours. We sat there having a snack and sipping at the hotel manager's spirit. There was no question of spending the night in the hut; we felt we could reach the hotel before dark, and in any case we had torches.

The steepness of the mountain suited me as I found it easy to descend by lowering myself with my arms. After ten hours of climbing I was beginning to tire and Eddy twice called a halt for a rest.

"There is no hurry," he advised. "Just concentrate."

While we sat and admired the view he said, "You should not push yourself so hard. You enjoy the mountains and perhaps ten hours is enough for you in a day."

"Perhaps a bit longer, depending on the sort of route. And routes like this are certainly easier for me, yard for yard, than snow routes."

My apprenticeship had been fully served. Now I knew how long I could best manage on different types of mountain terrain and I knew the sort of situations which were best avoided. Snow shoes, ski-baskets, the right boots, with plates and knee-pads for harder climbing: all helped to solve some of my particular problems. My stumps were toughened, and difficulties I had faced on earlier climbs such as the Jungfrau and Mont Blanc would not trouble me in the future. My reasonable limits had been defined.

Down again, down, down, steady, down, steady, concentrate. Down a hundred feet, two hundred, four hundred, seven hundred, a thousand. We drew close to the hotel, where a small group of climbers waited to congratulate our party. Night did not overtake us: we were back in the hotel at six thirty p.m., twenty minutes before darkness. The round trip had taken thirteen and a half hours, and I could have carried on for a few extra hours if it had been necessary. Soon only a dim outline of the mountain remained. I watched it for a long time. Had I really climbed up that shadow?

I felt very guilty at not being able to touch the special meal which the manager's wife cooked for us, but I could not keep anything down. I must be one of the few people in the world to have celebrated a climb with a glass of hot water. There I sat, quite tired, rather sick, and above all, delighted.

Miriam, Frau Biner and Jon rang to congratulate us all. Before long I went to bed. The only damage to my stumps was one abrasion about the size of the nail of my small finger.

By half past six the next day we were up and breakfasting. The two men who had been caught out by darkness had bivouacked above the hotel and descended safely at dawn.

Richard and Leo hurried down to the valley while Eddy, Götz and I went more slowly.

What followed then? A welcome bath at the Bahnhof Hotel, half a dozen cups of tea with Miriam and Jon in the kitchen, the warmth of their sincere congratulations, some wine with Eddy and Jon, plenty of big meals, a telephone call to Judy, who was delighted. Now I could go home.

Miriam and Jon saw me off at Zermatt station. It was growing dark as the train trundled down the valley but I could still see the fresh snow which lay in a continuous carpet down to seven thousand feet. The following day I would be thirty-four years old, and I felt more like eighteen. I was overwhelmed with feeling, with the wonderful taste of success. The ambitions were behind and I could go and climb without such single-mindedness. Trail walks, glacier treks, beautiful mountains: all were waiting. Yet despite feeling so young it was as if I had already lived one life, in a hurry. Any more would be a bonus.

The Wellenkuppe, the Mönch, the Jungfrau, the Breithorn, Mont Blanc, the Eiger, the Matterhorn: they are my dear friends who have let me taste life at its sweetest. I have memories which cannot be taken away, and what better treasures could I hope for? I am indeed a rich man.

NOTE

Obviously climbing will be suitable for only a minority of disabled people. The British Sports Association for the Disabled and the Disabled Living Foundation between them promote a wide range of other sports, and both are in need of funds to continue and expand their work. With a donation you could help ensure that other disabled people can enjoy something of the thrill which I have found through sport and tried to describe in this book.

British Sports Association for the Disabled,
Stoke Mandeville Sports Stadium,
Harvey Road,
Aylesbury,
Bucks HP21 8PP

Disabled Living Foundation,
346 Kensington High Street,
London W14 8NS